# 2023
# DAILY PLANNER

---

## PERSONAL INFORMATION

Name:

Address:

City:  State:  Zip:

Mobile Phone:  Home Phone:

Work Phone:

# 2023

## January 2023

| S | M | T | W | TH | F | S |
|---|---|---|---|----|---|---|
| 1 | 2 | 3 | 4 | 5 | 6 | 7 |
| 8 | 9 | 10 | 11 | 12 | 13 | 14 |
| 15 | 16 | 17 | 18 | 19 | 20 | 21 |
| 22 | 23 | 24 | 25 | 26 | 27 | 28 |
| 29 | 30 | 31 | | | | |

## February 2023

| S | M | T | W | TH | F | S |
|---|---|---|---|----|---|---|
| | | | 1 | 2 | 3 | 4 |
| 5 | 6 | 7 | 8 | 9 | 10 | 11 |
| 12 | 13 | 14 | 15 | 16 | 17 | 18 |
| 19 | 20 | 21 | 22 | 23 | 24 | 25 |
| 26 | 27 | 28 | | | | |

## March 2023

| S | M | T | W | TH | F | S |
|---|---|---|---|----|---|---|
| | | | 1 | 2 | 3 | 4 |
| 5 | 6 | 7 | 8 | 9 | 10 | 11 |
| 12 | 13 | 14 | 15 | 16 | 17 | 18 |
| 19 | 20 | 21 | 22 | 23 | 24 | 25 |
| 26 | 27 | 28 | 29 | 30 | 31 | |

## April 2023

| S | M | T | W | TH | F | S |
|---|---|---|---|----|---|---|
| | | | | | | 1 |
| 2 | 3 | 4 | 5 | 6 | 7 | 8 |
| 9 | 10 | 11 | 12 | 13 | 14 | 15 |
| 16 | 17 | 18 | 19 | 20 | 21 | 22 |
| 23 | 24 | 25 | 26 | 27 | 28 | 29 |
| 30 | | | | | | |

## May 2023

| S | M | T | W | TH | F | S |
|---|---|---|---|----|---|---|
| | 1 | 2 | 3 | 4 | 5 | 6 |
| 7 | 8 | 9 | 10 | 11 | 12 | 13 |
| 14 | 15 | 16 | 17 | 18 | 19 | 20 |
| 21 | 22 | 23 | 24 | 25 | 26 | 27 |
| 28 | 29 | 30 | 31 | | | |

## June 2023

| S | M | T | W | TH | F | S |
|---|---|---|---|----|---|---|
| | | | | 1 | 2 | 3 |
| 4 | 5 | 6 | 7 | 8 | 9 | 10 |
| 11 | 12 | 13 | 14 | 15 | 16 | 17 |
| 18 | 19 | 20 | 21 | 22 | 23 | 24 |
| 25 | 26 | 27 | 28 | 29 | 30 | |

## July 2023

| S | M | T | W | TH | F | S |
|---|---|---|---|----|---|---|
| | | | | | | 1 |
| 2 | 3 | 4 | 5 | 6 | 7 | 8 |
| 9 | 10 | 11 | 12 | 13 | 14 | 15 |
| 16 | 17 | 18 | 19 | 20 | 21 | 22 |
| 23 | 24 | 25 | 26 | 27 | 28 | 29 |
| 30 | 31 | | | | | |

## August 2023

| S | M | T | W | TH | F | S |
|---|---|---|---|----|---|---|
| | | 1 | 2 | 3 | 4 | 5 |
| 6 | 7 | 8 | 9 | 10 | 11 | 12 |
| 13 | 14 | 15 | 16 | 17 | 18 | 19 |
| 20 | 21 | 22 | 23 | 24 | 25 | 26 |
| 27 | 28 | 29 | 30 | 31 | | |

## September 2023

| S | M | T | W | TH | F | S |
|---|---|---|---|----|---|---|
| | | | | | 1 | 2 |
| 3 | 4 | 5 | 6 | 7 | 8 | 9 |
| 10 | 11 | 12 | 13 | 14 | 15 | 16 |
| 17 | 18 | 19 | 20 | 21 | 22 | 23 |
| 24 | 25 | 26 | 27 | 28 | 29 | 30 |

## October 2023

| S | M | T | W | TH | F | S |
|---|---|---|---|----|---|---|
| 1 | 2 | 3 | 4 | 5 | 6 | 7 |
| 8 | 9 | 10 | 11 | 12 | 13 | 14 |
| 15 | 16 | 17 | 18 | 19 | 20 | 21 |
| 22 | 23 | 24 | 25 | 26 | 27 | 28 |
| 29 | 30 | 31 | | | | |

## November 2023

| S | M | T | W | TH | F | S |
|---|---|---|---|----|---|---|
| | | | 1 | 2 | 3 | 4 |
| 5 | 6 | 7 | 8 | 9 | 10 | 11 |
| 12 | 13 | 14 | 15 | 16 | 17 | 18 |
| 19 | 20 | 21 | 22 | 23 | 24 | 25 |
| 26 | 27 | 28 | 29 | 30 | | |

## December 2023

| S | M | T | W | TH | F | S |
|---|---|---|---|----|---|---|
| | | | | | 1 | 2 |
| 3 | 4 | 5 | 6 | 7 | 8 | 9 |
| 10 | 11 | 12 | 13 | 14 | 15 | 16 |
| 17 | 18 | 19 | 20 | 21 | 22 | 23 |
| 24 | 25 | 26 | 27 | 28 | 29 | 30 |
| 31 | | | | | | |

*Let the morning bring me word of your unfailing love,*
*for I have put my trust in you. Show me the way I*
*should go, for to you I entrust my life.*

PSALM 143:8

# 2024

| January 2024 | February 2024 | March 2024 |
|---|---|---|

**January 2024**

| S | M | T | W | TH | F | S |
|---|---|---|---|---|---|---|
|  | 1 | 2 | 3 | 4 | 5 | 6 |
| 7 | 8 | 9 | 10 | 11 | 12 | 13 |
| 14 | 15 | 16 | 17 | 18 | 19 | 20 |
| 21 | 22 | 23 | 24 | 25 | 26 | 27 |
| 28 | 29 | 30 | 31 |  |  |  |

**February 2024**

| S | M | T | W | TH | F | S |
|---|---|---|---|---|---|---|
|  |  |  |  | 1 | 2 | 3 |
| 4 | 5 | 6 | 7 | 8 | 9 | 10 |
| 11 | 12 | 13 | 14 | 15 | 16 | 17 |
| 18 | 19 | 20 | 21 | 22 | 23 | 24 |
| 25 | 26 | 27 | 28 | 29 |  |  |

**March 2024**

| S | M | T | W | TH | F | S |
|---|---|---|---|---|---|---|
|  |  |  |  |  | 1 | 2 |
| 3 | 4 | 5 | 6 | 7 | 8 | 9 |
| 10 | 11 | 12 | 13 | 14 | 15 | 16 |
| 17 | 18 | 19 | 20 | 21 | 22 | 23 |
| 24 | 25 | 26 | 27 | 28 | 29 | 30 |
| 31 |  |  |  |  |  |  |

**April 2024**

| S | M | T | W | TH | F | S |
|---|---|---|---|---|---|---|
|  | 1 | 2 | 3 | 4 | 5 | 6 |
| 7 | 8 | 9 | 10 | 11 | 12 | 13 |
| 14 | 15 | 16 | 17 | 18 | 19 | 20 |
| 21 | 22 | 23 | 24 | 25 | 26 | 27 |
| 28 | 29 | 30 |  |  |  |  |

**May 2024**

| S | M | T | W | TH | F | S |
|---|---|---|---|---|---|---|
|  |  |  | 1 | 2 | 3 | 4 |
| 5 | 6 | 7 | 8 | 9 | 10 | 11 |
| 12 | 13 | 14 | 15 | 16 | 17 | 18 |
| 19 | 20 | 21 | 22 | 23 | 24 | 25 |
| 26 | 27 | 28 | 29 | 30 | 31 |  |

**June 2024**

| S | M | T | W | TH | F | S |
|---|---|---|---|---|---|---|
|  |  |  |  |  |  | 1 |
| 2 | 3 | 4 | 5 | 6 | 7 | 8 |
| 9 | 10 | 11 | 12 | 13 | 14 | 15 |
| 16 | 17 | 18 | 19 | 20 | 21 | 22 |
| 23 | 24 | 25 | 26 | 27 | 28 | 29 |
| 30 |  |  |  |  |  |  |

**July 2024**

| S | M | T | W | TH | F | S |
|---|---|---|---|---|---|---|
|  | 1 | 2 | 3 | 4 | 5 | 6 |
| 7 | 8 | 9 | 10 | 11 | 12 | 13 |
| 14 | 15 | 16 | 17 | 18 | 19 | 20 |
| 21 | 22 | 23 | 24 | 25 | 26 | 27 |
| 28 | 29 | 30 | 31 |  |  |  |

**August 2024**

| S | M | T | W | TH | F | S |
|---|---|---|---|---|---|---|
|  |  |  |  | 1 | 2 | 3 |
| 4 | 5 | 6 | 7 | 8 | 9 | 10 |
| 11 | 12 | 13 | 14 | 15 | 16 | 17 |
| 18 | 19 | 20 | 21 | 22 | 23 | 24 |
| 25 | 26 | 27 | 28 | 29 | 30 | 31 |

**September 2024**

| S | M | T | W | TH | F | S |
|---|---|---|---|---|---|---|
| 1 | 2 | 3 | 4 | 5 | 6 | 7 |
| 8 | 9 | 10 | 11 | 12 | 13 | 14 |
| 15 | 16 | 17 | 18 | 19 | 20 | 21 |
| 22 | 23 | 24 | 25 | 26 | 27 | 28 |
| 29 | 30 |  |  |  |  |  |

**October 2024**

| S | M | T | W | TH | F | S |
|---|---|---|---|---|---|---|
|  |  | 1 | 2 | 3 | 4 | 5 |
| 6 | 7 | 8 | 9 | 10 | 11 | 12 |
| 13 | 14 | 15 | 16 | 17 | 18 | 19 |
| 20 | 21 | 22 | 23 | 24 | 25 | 26 |
| 27 | 28 | 29 | 30 | 31 |  |  |

**November 2024**

| S | M | T | W | TH | F | S |
|---|---|---|---|---|---|---|
|  |  |  |  |  | 1 | 2 |
| 3 | 4 | 5 | 6 | 7 | 8 | 9 |
| 10 | 11 | 12 | 13 | 14 | 15 | 16 |
| 17 | 18 | 19 | 20 | 21 | 22 | 23 |
| 24 | 25 | 26 | 27 | 28 | 29 | 30 |

**December 2024**

| S | M | T | W | TH | F | S |
|---|---|---|---|---|---|---|
| 1 | 2 | 3 | 4 | 5 | 6 | 7 |
| 8 | 9 | 10 | 11 | 12 | 13 | 14 |
| 15 | 16 | 17 | 18 | 19 | 20 | 21 |
| 22 | 23 | 24 | 25 | 26 | 27 | 28 |
| 29 | 30 | 31 |  |  |  |  |

*"No human mind has conceived"—the things God has prepared for those who love him.*

1 CORINTHIANS 2:9

# Bible Reading Schedule

**JANUARY**

1  Gen. 1–3; Mt. 1
2  Gen. 4–6; Mt. 2
3  Gen. 7–9; Mt. 3
4  Gen. 10–12; Mt. 4
5  Gen. 13–15; Mt. 5:1–26
6  Gen. 16–17; Mt. 5:27–48
7  Gen. 18–19; Mt. 6:1–18
8  Gen. 20–22; Mt. 6:19–34
9  Gen. 23–24; Mt. 7
10  Gen. 25–26; Mt. 8:1–17
11  Gen. 27–28; Mt. 8:18–34
12  Gen. 29–30; Mt. 9:1–17
13  Gen. 31–32; Mt. 9:18–38
14  Gen. 33–35; Mt. 10:1–20
15  Gen. 36–38; Mt. 10:21–42
16  Gen. 39–40; Mt. 11
17  Gen. 41–42; Mt. 12:1–23
18  Gen. 43–45; Mt. 12:24–50
19  Gen. 46–48; Mt. 13:1–30
20  Gen. 49–50; Mt. 13:31–58
21  Ex. 1–3; Mt. 14:1–21
22  Ex. 4–6; Mt. 14:22–36
23  Ex. 7–8; Mt. 15:1–20
24  Ex. 9–11; Mt. 15:21–39
25  Ex. 12–13; Mt. 16
26  Ex. 14–15; Mt. 17
27  Ex. 16–18; Mt. 18:1–20
28  Ex. 19–20; Mt. 18:21–35
29  Ex. 21–22; Mt. 19
30  Ex. 23–24; Mt. 20:1–16
31  Ex. 25–26; Mt. 20:17–34

**FEBRUARY**

1  Ex. 27–28; Mt. 21:1–22
2  Ex. 29–30; Mt. 21:23–46
3  Ex. 31–33; Mt. 22:1–22
4  Ex. 34–35; Mt. 22:23–46
5  Ex. 36–38; Mt. 23:1–22
6  Ex. 39–40; Mt. 23:23–39
7  Lev. 1–3; Mt. 24:1–28
8  Lev. 4–5; Mt. 24:29–51
9  Lev. 6–7; Mt. 25:1–30
10  Lev. 8–10; Mt. 25:31–46
11  Lev. 11–12; Mt. 26:1–25
12  Lev. 13; Mt. 26:26–50
13  Lev. 14; Mt. 26:51–75
14  Lev. 15–16; Mt. 27:1–26

15  Lev. 17–18; Mt. 27:27–50
16  Lev. 19–20; Mt. 27:51–66
17  Lev. 21–22; Mt. 28
18  Lev. 23–24; Mk. 1:1–22
19  Lev. 25; Mk. 1:23–45
20  Lev. 26–27; Mk. 2
21  Num. 1–3; Mk. 3
22  Num. 4–6; Mk. 4:1–20
23  Num. 7–8; Mk. 4:21–41
24  Num. 9–11; Mk. 5:1–20
25  Num. 12–14; Mk. 5:21–43
26  Num. 15–16; Mk. 6:1–29
27  Num. 17–19; Mk. 6:30–56
28  Num. 20–22; Mk. 7:1–13

**MARCH**

1  Num. 23–25; Mk. 7:14–37
2  Num. 26–27; Mk. 8:1–21
3  Num. 28–30; Mk. 8:22–38
4  Num. 31–33; Mk. 9:1–29
5  Num. 34–36; Mk. 9:30–50
6  Dt. 1–2; Mk. 10:1–31
7  Dt. 3–4; Mk. 10:32–52
8  Dt. 5–7; Mk. 11:1–18
9  Dt. 8–10; Mk. 11:19–33
10  Dt. 11–13; Mk. 12:1–27
11  Dt. 14–16; Mk. 12:28–44
12  Dt. 17–19; Mk. 13:1–20
13  Dt. 20–22; Mk. 13:21–37
14  Dt. 23–25; Mk. 14:1–26
15  Dt. 26–27; Mk. 14:27–53
16  Dt. 28–29; Mk. 14:54–72
17  Dt. 30–31; Mk. 15:1–25
18  Dt. 32–34; Mk. 15:26–47
19  Josh. 1–3; Mk. 16
20  Josh. 4–6; Lk. 1:1–20
21  Josh. 7–9; Lk. 1:21–38
22  Josh. 10–12; Lk. 1:39–56
23  Josh. 13–15; Lk. 1:57–80
24  Josh. 16–18; Lk. 2:1–24
25  Josh. 19–21; Lk. 2:25–52
26  Josh. 22–24; Lk. 3
27  Jud. 1–3; Lk. 4:1–30
28  Jud. 4–6; Lk. 4:31–44
29  Jud. 7–8; Lk. 5:1–16
30  Jud. 9–10; Lk. 5:17–39
31  Jud. 11–12; Lk. 6:1–26

# Bible Reading Schedule

**APRIL**

- 1 Jud. 13–15; Lk. 6:27–49
- 2 Jud. 16–18; Lk. 7:1–30
- 3 Jud. 19–21; Lk. 7:31–50
- 4 Ruth 1–4; Lk. 8:1–25
- 5 1 Sam. 1–3; Lk. 8:26–56
- 6 1 Sam. 4–6; Lk. 9:1–17
- 7 1 Sam. 7–9; Lk. 9:18–36
- 8 1 Sam. 10–12; Lk. 9:37–62
- 9 1 Sam. 13–14; Lk. 10:1–24
- 10 1 Sam. 15–16; Lk. 10:25–42
- 11 1 Sam. 17–18; Lk. 11:1–28
- 12 1 Sam. 19–21; Lk. 11:29–54
- 13 1 Sam. 22–24; Lk. 12:1–31
- 14 1 Sam. 25–26; Lk. 12:32–59
- 15 1 Sam. 27–29; Lk. 13:1–22
- 16 1 Sam. 30–31; Lk. 13:23–35
- 17 2 Sam. 1–2; Lk. 14:1–24
- 18 2 Sam. 3–5; Lk. 14:25–35
- 19 2 Sam. 6–8; Lk. 15:1–10
- 20 2 Sam. 9–11; Lk. 15:11–32
- 21 2 Sam. 12–13; Lk. 16
- 22 2 Sam. 14–15; Lk. 17:1–19
- 23 2 Sam. 16–18; Lk. 17:20–37
- 24 2 Sam. 19–20; Lk. 18:1–23
- 25 2 Sam. 21–22; Lk. 18:24–43
- 26 2 Sam. 23–24; Lk. 19:1–27
- 27 1 Ki. 1–2; Lk. 19:28–48
- 28 1 Ki. 3–5; Lk. 20:1–26
- 29 1 Ki. 6–7; Lk. 20:27–47
- 30 1 Ki. 8–9; Lk. 21:1–19

**MAY**

- 1 1 Ki. 10–11; Lk. 21:20–38
- 2 1 Ki. 12–13; Lk. 22:1–20
- 3 1 Ki. 14–15; Lk. 22:21–46
- 4 1 Ki. 16–18; Lk. 22:47–71
- 5 1 Ki. 19–20; Lk. 23:1–25
- 6 1 Ki. 21–22; Lk. 23:26–56
- 7 2 Ki. 1–3; Lk. 24:1–35
- 8 2 Ki. 4–6; Lk. 24:36–53
- 9 2 Ki. 7–9; Jn. 1:1–28
- 10 2 Ki. 10–12; Jn. 1:29–51
- 11 2 Ki. 13–14; Jn. 2
- 12 2 Ki. 15–16; Jn. 3:1–18
- 13 2 Ki. 17–18; Jn. 3:19–36
- 14 2 Ki. 19–21; Jn. 4:1–30
- 15 2 Ki. 22–23; Jn. 4:31–54
- 16 2 Ki. 24–25; Jn. 5:1–24
- 17 1 Chr. 1–3; Jn. 5:25–47
- 18 1 Chr. 4–6; Jn. 6:1–21
- 19 1 Chr. 7–9; Jn. 6:22–44
- 20 1 Chr. 10–12; Jn. 6:45–71
- 21 1 Chr. 13–15; Jn. 7:1–27
- 22 1 Chr. 16–18; Jn. 7:28–53
- 23 1 Chr. 19–21; Jn. 8:1–27
- 24 1 Chr. 22–24; Jn. 8:28–59
- 25 1 Chr. 25–27; Jn. 9:1–23
- 26 1 Chr. 28–29; Jn. 9:24–41
- 27 2 Chr. 1–3; Jn. 10:1–23
- 28 2 Chr. 4–6; Jn. 10:24–42
- 29 2 Chr. 7–9; Jn. 11:1–29
- 30 2 Chr. 10–12; Jn. 11:30–57
- 31 2 Chr. 13–14; Jn. 12:1–26

**JUNE**

- 1 2 Chr. 15–16; Jn. 12:27–50
- 2 2 Chr. 17–18; Jn. 13:1–20
- 3 2 Chr. 19–20; Jn. 13:21–38
- 4 2 Chr. 21–22; Jn. 14
- 5 2 Chr. 23–24; Jn. 15
- 6 2 Chr. 25–27; Jn. 16
- 7 2 Chr. 28–29; Jn. 17
- 8 2 Chr. 30–31; Jn. 18:1–18
- 9 2 Chr. 32–33; Jn. 18:19–40
- 10 2 Chr. 34–36; Jn. 19:1–22
- 11 Ezra 1–2; Jn. 19:23–42
- 12 Ezra 3–5; Jn. 20
- 13 Ezra 6–8; Jn. 21
- 14 Ezra 9–10; Acts 1
- 15 Neh. 1–3; Acts 2:1–21
- 16 Neh. 4–6; Acts 2:22–47
- 17 Neh. 7–9; Acts 3
- 18 Neh. 10–11; Acts 4:1–22
- 19 Neh. 12–13; Acts 4:23–37
- 20 Est. 1–2; Acts 5:1–21
- 21 Est. 3–5; Acts 5:22–42
- 22 Est. 6–8; Acts 6
- 23 Est. 9–10; Acts 7:1–21
- 24 Job 1–2; Acts 7:22–43
- 25 Job 3–4; Acts 7:44–60
- 26 Job 5–7; Acts 8:1–25
- 27 Job 8–10; Acts 8:26–40
- 28 Job 11–13; Acts 9:1–21
- 29 Job 14–16; Acts 9:22–43
- 30 Job 17–19; Acts 10:1–23

# Bible Reading Schedule

**JULY**

1   Job 20–21; Acts 10:24–48
2   Job 22–24; Acts 11
3   Job 25–27; Acts 12
4   Job 28–29; Acts 13:1–25
5   Job 30–31; Acts 13:26–52
6   Job 32–33; Acts 14
7   Job 34–35; Acts 15:1–21
8   Job 36–37; Acts 15:22–41
9   Job 38–40; Acts 16:1–21
10   Job 41–42; Acts 16:22–40
11   Ps. 1–3; Acts 17:1–15
12   Ps. 4–6; Acts 17:16–34
13   Ps. 7–9; Acts 18
14   Ps. 10–12; Acts 19:1–20
15   Ps. 13–15; Acts 19:21–41
16   Ps. 16–17; Acts 20:1–16
17   Ps. 18–19; Acts 20:17–38
18   Ps. 20–22; Acts 21:1–17
19   Ps. 23–25; Acts 21:18–40
20   Ps. 26–28; Acts 22
21   Ps. 29–30; Acts 23:1–15
22   Ps. 31–32; Acts 23:16–35
23   Ps. 33–34; Acts 24
24   Ps. 35–36; Acts 25
25   Ps. 37–39; Acts 26
26   Ps. 40–42; Acts 27:1–26
27   Ps. 43–45; Acts 27:27–44
28   Ps. 46–48; Acts 28
29   Ps. 49–50; Rom. 1
30   Ps. 51–53; Rom. 2
31   Ps. 54–56; Rom. 3

**AUGUST**

1   Ps. 57–59; Rom. 4
2   Ps. 60–62; Rom. 5
3   Ps. 63–65; Rom. 6
4   Ps. 66–67; Rom. 7
5   Ps. 68–69; Rom. 8:1–21
6   Ps. 70–71; Rom. 8:22–39
7   Ps. 72–73; Rom. 9:1–15
8   Ps. 74–76; Rom. 9:16–33
9   Ps. 77–78; Rom. 10
10   Ps. 79–80; Rom. 11:1–18
11   Ps. 81–83; Rom. 11:19–36
12   Ps. 84–86; Rom. 12
13   Ps. 87–88; Rom. 13
14   Ps. 89–90; Rom. 14
15   Ps. 91–93; Rom. 15:1–13
16   Ps. 94–96; Rom. 15:14–33
17   Ps. 97–99; Rom. 16
18   Ps. 100–102; 1 Cor. 1
19   Ps. 103–104; 1 Cor. 2
20   Ps. 105–106; 1 Cor. 3
21   Ps. 107–109; 1 Cor. 4
22   Ps. 110–112; 1 Cor. 5
23   Ps. 113–115; 1 Cor. 6
24   Ps. 116–118; 1 Cor. 7:1–19
25   Ps. 119:1–88; 1 Cor. 7:20–40
26   Ps. 119:89–176; 1 Cor. 8
27   Ps. 120–122; 1 Cor. 9
28   Ps. 123–125; 1 Cor. 10:1–18
29   Ps. 126–128; 1 Cor. 10:19–33
30   Ps. 129–131; 1 Cor. 11:1–16
31   Ps. 132–134; 1 Cor. 11:17–34

**SEPTEMBER**

1   Ps. 135–136; 1 Cor. 12
2   Ps. 137–139; 1 Cor. 13
3   Ps. 140–142; 1 Cor. 14:1–20
4   Ps. 143–145; 1 Cor. 14:21–40
5   Ps. 146–147; 1 Cor. 15:1–28
6   Ps. 148–150; 1 Cor. 15:29–58
7   Prov. 1–2; 1 Cor. 16
8   Prov. 3–5; 2 Cor. 1
9   Prov. 6–7; 2 Cor. 2
10   Prov. 8–9; 2 Cor. 3
11   Prov. 10–12; 2 Cor. 4
12   Prov. 13–15; 2 Cor. 5
13   Prov. 16–18; 2 Cor. 6
14   Prov. 19–21; 2 Cor. 7
15   Prov. 22–24; 2 Cor. 8
16   Prov. 25–26; 2 Cor. 9
17   Prov. 27–29; 2 Cor. 10
18   Prov. 30–31; 2 Cor. 11:1–15
19   Eccl. 1–3; 2 Cor. 11:16–33
20   Eccl. 4–6; 2 Cor. 12
21   Eccl. 7–9; 2 Cor. 13
22   Eccl. 10–12; Gal. 1
23   Song 1–3; Gal. 2
24   Song 4–5; Gal. 3
25   Song 6–8; Gal. 4
26   Isa. 1–2; Gal. 5
27   Isa. 3–4; Gal. 6
28   Isa. 5–6; Eph. 1
29   Isa. 7–8; Eph. 2
30   Isa. 9–10; Eph. 3

# Bible Reading Schedule

**OCTOBER**

1   Isa. 11–13; Eph. 4
2   Isa. 14–16; Eph. 5:1–16
3   Isa. 17–19; Eph. 5:17–33
4   Isa. 20–22; Eph. 6
5   Isa. 23–25; Phil. 1
6   Isa. 26–27; Phil. 2
7   Isa. 28–29; Phil. 3
8   Isa. 30–31; Phil 4
9   Isa. 32–33; Col. 1
10   Isa. 34–36; Col. 2
11   Isa. 37–38; Col. 3
12   Isa. 39–40; Col. 4
13   Isa. 41–42; 1 Th. 1
14   Isa. 43–44; 1 Th. 2
15   Isa. 45–46; 1 Th. 3
16   Isa. 47–49; 1 Th. 4
17   Isa. 50–52; 1 Th. 5
18   Isa. 53–55; 2 Th. 1
19   Isa. 56–58; 2 Th. 2
20   Isa. 59–61; 2 Th. 3
21   Isa. 62–64; 1 Tim. 1
22   Isa. 65–66; 1 Tim. 2
23   Jer. 1–2; 1 Tim. 3
24   Jer. 3–5; 1 Tim. 4
25   Jer. 6–8; 1 Tim. 5
26   Jer. 9–11; 1 Tim. 6
27   Jer. 12–14; 2 Tim. 1
28   Jer. 15–17; 2 Tim. 2
29   Jer. 18–19; 2 Tim. 3
30   Jer. 20–21; 2 Tim. 4
31   Jer. 22–23; Ti. 1

**NOVEMBER**

1   Jer. 24–26; Ti. 2
2   Jer. 27–29; Ti. 3
3   Jer. 30–31; Philemon
4   Jer. 32–33; Heb. 1
5   Jer. 34–36; Heb. 2
6   Jer. 37–39; Heb. 3
7   Jer. 40–42; Heb. 4
8   Jer. 43–45; Heb. 5
9   Jer. 46–47; Heb. 6
10   Jer. 48–49; Heb. 7
11   Jer. 50; Heb. 8
12   Jer. 51–52; Heb. 9
13   Lam. 1–2; Heb. 10:1–18
14   Lam. 3–5; Heb. 10:19–39
15   Ezek. 1–2; Heb. 11:1–19
16   Ezek. 3–4; Heb. 11:20–40
17   Ezek. 5–7; Heb. 12
18   Ezek. 8–10; Heb. 13
19   Ezek. 11–13; Jas. 1
20   Ezek. 14–15; Jas. 2
21   Ezek. 16–17; Jas. 3
22   Ezek. 18–19; Jas. 4
23   Ezek. 20–21; Jas. 5
24   Ezek. 22–23; 1 Pet. 1
25   Ezek. 24–26; 1 Pet. 2
26   Ezek. 27–29; 1 Pet. 3
27   Ezek. 30–32; 1 Pet. 4
28   Ezek. 33–34; 1 Pet. 5
29   Ezek. 35–36; 2 Pet. 1
30   Ezek. 37–39; 2 Pet. 2

**DECEMBER**

1   Ezek. 40–41; 2 Pet. 3
2   Ezek. 42–44; 1 Jn. 1
3   Ezek. 45–46; 1 Jn. 2
4   Ezek. 47–48; 1 Jn. 3
5   Dan. 1–2; 1 Jn. 4
6   Dan. 3–4; 1 Jn. 5
7   Dan. 5–7; 2 John
8   Dan. 8–10; 3 John
9   Dan. 11–12; Jude
10   Hos. 1–4; Rev. 1
11   Hos. 5–8; Rev. 2
12   Hos. 9–11; Rev. 3
13   Hos. 12–14; Rev. 4
14   Joel 1–3; Rev. 5
15   Amos 1–3; Rev. 6
16   Amos 4–6; Rev. 7
17   Amos 7–9; Rev. 8
18   Obadiah; Rev. 9
19   Jonah 1–4; Rev. 10
20   Mic. 1–3; Rev. 11
21   Mic. 4–5; Rev. 12
22   Mic. 6–7; Rev. 13
23   Nahum 1–3; Rev. 14
24   Habakkuk 1–3; Rev. 15
25   Zephaniah 1–3; Rev. 16
26   Haggai 1–2; Rev. 17
27   Zech. 1–4; Rev. 18
28   Zech. 5–8; Rev. 19
29   Zech. 9–12; Rev. 20
30   Zech. 13–14; Rev. 21
31   Malachi 1–4; Rev. 22

# When Compassion Wins

*A Samaritan, as he traveled, came where the man was; and when he saw him, he took pity on him.*  LUKE 10:33

Ashanti was concerned for a stranger on Chicago's Red Line elevated train. "Can I pray for you?" he asked. The fellow commuter's sunglasses couldn't cover her distress. Though a scheduled meeting was beckoning Ashanti, the heart-pull to respond to the person before him was stronger. At the end of his prayer, the woman responded, "I'm an atheist." But she also expressed that Ashanti's compassion had caused her to ponder her unbelief.

Have you had to choose between taking the path of least resistance or stretching yourself to do the uncomfortable but right thing? You're not alone. The story that Jesus told in Luke 10:29–37 compels us to rethink our fears, prejudices, and complacencies.

We don't know how the Samaritan in Jesus' story processed his decision to help the presumed Jewish traveler who'd fallen into the hands of thieves and robbers (v. 30). What we do know is that those who had the reputation for being the "good guys" passed up the opportunity to help one who desperately needed it. Compassion came through one who for centuries had been considered an ethnic and religious outsider (see John 4:1–9). "But a Samaritan, as he traveled, came where the man was; and when he saw him, he took pity on him" (v. 33). When compassion wins, everybody wins—givers and receivers. In this new year, let's move forward in *compassion as God guides us.*  ARTHUR JACKSON

# JANUARY

| Sunday | Monday | Tuesday | Wednesday |
|---|---|---|---|
| 1<br><br>New Year's Day | 2 | 3 | 4 |
| 8 | 9 | 10 | 11 |
| 15 | 16<br><br>Martin Luther King Jr. Day | 17 | 18 |
| 22 | 23 | 24 | 25 |
| 29 | 30 | 31 | |

*How beautiful on the mountains are the feet of those
who bring good news, who proclaim peace, who bring
good tidings, who proclaim salvation.* —ISAIAH 52:7

| Thursday | Friday | Saturday | Notes |
|---|---|---|---|
| 5 | 6 | 7 | |
| | Epiphany | | |
| 12 | 13 | 14 | |
| 19 | 20 | 21 | |
| 26 | 27 | 28 | |
| | | | |

## Shopping List

✓

# 2023

# JANUARY

**Sunday 1** New Year's Day

**Monday 2**

**Tuesday 3**

**Wednesday** 4

**Thursday** 5

**Friday** 6 Epiphany

**Saturday** 7

To-Do List

<table>
<tr><td>

## Shopping List

✓

</td><td>

| January 2023 | | | | | | |
|---|---|---|---|---|---|---|
| **S** | **M** | **T** | **W** | **TH** | **F** | **S** |
| 1 | 2 | 3 | 4 | 5 | 6 | 7 |
| 8 | 9 | 10 | 11 | 12 | 13 | 14 |
| 15 | 16 | 17 | 18 | 19 | 20 | 21 |
| 22 | 23 | 24 | 25 | 26 | 27 | 28 |
| 29 | 30 | 31 | | | | |

| February 2023 | | | | | | |
|---|---|---|---|---|---|---|
| **S** | **M** | **T** | **W** | **TH** | **F** | **S** |
| | | | 1 | 2 | 3 | 4 |
| 5 | 6 | 7 | 8 | 9 | 10 | 11 |
| 12 | 13 | 14 | 15 | 16 | 17 | 18 |
| 19 | 20 | 21 | 22 | 23 | 24 | 25 |
| 26 | 27 | 28 | | | | |

## 2023
# JANUARY

**Sunday 8**

**Monday 9**

**Tuesday 10**

</td></tr>
</table>

**Wednesday** 11

**Thursday** 12

**Friday** 13

**Saturday** 14

To-Do List

✓

## Shopping List

✓

### 2023

# JANUARY

**Sunday** 15

**Monday** 16   Martin Luther King Jr. Day

**Tuesday** 17

**Wednesday** 18

**Thursday** 19

**Friday** 20

**Saturday** 21

## To-Do List

✓

## Shopping List

2023

# JANUARY

**Sunday** 22

**Monday** 23

**Tuesday** 24

**Wednesday** 25

**Thursday** 26

**Friday** 27

**Saturday** 28

## To-Do List

✓

# Shrek the Sheep

*[We] were like sheep going astray.*
1 PETER 2:25

In 1998, Shrek, a New Zealand Merino sheep, escaped his shepherds and hid in mountainous caves. For six years, Shrek lived the wild and free life, but when they found him, he was unrecognizable, overheating, and struggling due to the enormous amount of wool he was carrying. In fact, the wool shorn off him was enough to create twenty large men suits. Back with the shepherds, the sheep could be truly free.

We also seek to be free. But if we wander from God we'll only find struggles, not freedom. Peter, quoting the prophet Isaiah, refers to God as our shepherd and recounts for us the tragic ways we (His sheep) have abandoned the One who watches over us. We "were like sheep going astray" (1 Peter 2:25). But in the harsh world, left to our own devices, we endured the consequences of our rebellion, the weight of our disastrous choices, the scars of our foolishness. Thankfully, God didn't leave us to ourselves but came to rescue us. By Jesus' "wounds [we] have been healed" (v.24). He's returned us "to the Shepherd . . . of [our] souls" (v.25).

When we return to our Shepherd, we discover that this is where true freedom exists. When we're with God, we're our truest selves as He cares for us and equips us to live out genuine, responsible liberty. With the Shepherd, we're free and loved.

WINN COLLIER

*Photo: Lake District, England*
*© Rick DeHaan*

# FEBRUARY

| Sunday | Monday | Tuesday | Wednesday |
|---|---|---|---|
| | | | 1 |
| 5 | 6 | 7 | 8 |
| 12 | 13 | 14<br>Valentine's Day | 15<br>Flag Day (Canada) |
| 19 | 20<br>Presidents' Day | 21 | 22<br>Ash Wednesday |
| 26 | 27 | 28 | |

| Thursday | Friday | Saturday | Notes |
|---|---|---|---|
| 2<br><br>Groundhog Day | 3 | 4 | |
| 9 | 10 | 11 | |
| 16 | 17 | 18 | |
| 23 | 24 | 25 | |
| | | | |

## Shopping List

| January 2023 | | | | | | |
|---|---|---|---|---|---|---|
| **S** | **M** | **T** | **W** | **TH** | **F** | **S** |
| 1 | 2 | 3 | 4 | 5 | 6 | 7 |
| 8 | 9 | 10 | 11 | 12 | 13 | 14 |
| 15 | 16 | 17 | 18 | 19 | 20 | 21 |
| 22 | 23 | 24 | 25 | 26 | 27 | 28 |
| 29 | 30 | 31 | | | | |

| February 2023 | | | | | | |
|---|---|---|---|---|---|---|
| **S** | **M** | **T** | **W** | **TH** | **F** | **S** |
| | | | 1 | 2 | 3 | 4 |
| 5 | 6 | 7 | 8 | 9 | 10 | 11 |
| 12 | 13 | 14 | 15 | 16 | 17 | 18 |
| 19 | 20 | 21 | 22 | 23 | 24 | 25 |
| 26 | 27 | 28 | | | | |

## 2023

# JAN–FEB

**Sunday** 29

**Monday** 30

**Tuesday** 31

**Wednesday** 1

---

**Thursday** 2 Groundhog Day

---

**Friday** 3

---

**Saturday** 4

## To-Do List

✓

## Shopping List

✓

# 2023

# FEBRUARY

**Sunday** 5

**Monday** 6

**Tuesday** 7

**Wednesday** 8

**Thursday** 9

**Friday** 10

**Saturday** 11

## To-Do List

✓

## Shopping List

✓

2023

# FEBRUARY

**Sunday** 12

**Monday** 13

**Tuesday** 14   Valentine's Day

**Wednesday 15**  Flag Day (Canada)

**Thursday 16**

**Friday 17**

**Saturday 18**

## To-Do List

✓

## Shopping List

<table>
<tr><th>✓</th><th></th></tr>
</table>

| February 2023 | | | | | | |
|---|---|---|---|---|---|---|
| S | M | T | W | TH | F | S |
| | | | 1 | 2 | 3 | 4 |
| 5 | 6 | 7 | 8 | 9 | 10 | 11 |
| 12 | 13 | 14 | 15 | 16 | 17 | 18 |
| 19 | 20 | 21 | 22 | 23 | 24 | 25 |
| 26 | 27 | 28 | | | | |

| March 2023 | | | | | | |
|---|---|---|---|---|---|---|
| S | M | T | W | TH | F | S |
| | | | 1 | 2 | 3 | 4 |
| 5 | 6 | 7 | 8 | 9 | 10 | 11 |
| 12 | 13 | 14 | 15 | 16 | 17 | 18 |
| 19 | 20 | 21 | 22 | 23 | 24 | 25 |
| 26 | 27 | 28 | 29 | 30 | 31 | |

# 2023

# FEBRUARY

**Sunday** 19

**Monday** 20 Presidents' Day

**Tuesday** 21

**Wednesday 22** Ash Wednesday

**Thursday 23**

**Friday 24**

**Saturday 25**

## To-Do List

✓

# Sea Glass

*We also glory in our sufferings, because we know that suffering produces perseverance; perseverance, character; and character, hope.* ROMANS 5:3–4

Walking along the coast of Maine, my daughters and I finally found what we were searching for in the wide expanse of sand. *Sea glass!* We raced to collect the treasure before the waters could sweep it back into the ocean.

Genuine sea glass is created when broken glass, perhaps from bottles or tableware, is discarded from ships out in the middle of vast bodies of water. After years of rolling and tumbling in the waves, the broken glass's rough edges are smoothed away and it takes on a beautiful frosted appearance.

Part of why I love sea glass is that each piece in my collection reminds me that God can create unexpected beauty out of even our greatest struggles. As Paul assured the Roman believers, "Suffering produces perseverance; perseverance, character; and character, hope" (Romans 5:3–4).

Through God's grace and power, even pain caused by a fallen world can be used in a refining process—one that deepens our dependence on Him and transforms us to be more like Christ (8:17).

That gives me great hope when I find myself battered by the waves and wind of life. And I eagerly await the day when we'll find ourselves—and *all* of God's creation (vv. 19–21)—fully renewed and transformed in a breathtaking display of His glory and grace. LISA SAMRA

*Photo: Patmos, Greece, in the Aegean Sea*
© Alex Soh

# MARCH

| Sunday | Monday | Tuesday | Wednesday |
|---|---|---|---|
| | | | 1 |
| 5 | 6 | 7<br>Purim | 8 |
| 12<br>Daylight Saving Time Begins | 13<br>Commonwealth Day (Canada) | 14 | 15 |
| 19 | 20<br>First Day of Spring | 21 | 22 |
| 26 | 27 | 28 | 29 |

| Thursday | Friday | Saturday | Notes |
|---|---|---|---|
| 2 | 3 | 4 | |
| 9 | 10 | 11 | |
| 16 | 17<br>St. Patrick's Day | 18 | |
| 23 | 24 | 25 | |
| 30 | 31 | | |

## Shopping List

| ✓ | |
|---|---|

<table>
<tr><th colspan="7">February 2023</th></tr>
<tr><th>S</th><th>M</th><th>T</th><th>W</th><th>TH</th><th>F</th><th>S</th></tr>
<tr><td></td><td></td><td></td><td>1</td><td>2</td><td>3</td><td>4</td></tr>
<tr><td>5</td><td>6</td><td>7</td><td>8</td><td>9</td><td>10</td><td>11</td></tr>
<tr><td>12</td><td>13</td><td>14</td><td>15</td><td>16</td><td>17</td><td>18</td></tr>
<tr><td>19</td><td>20</td><td>21</td><td>22</td><td>23</td><td>24</td><td>25</td></tr>
<tr><td>26</td><td>27</td><td>28</td><td></td><td></td><td></td><td></td></tr>
</table>

<table>
<tr><th colspan="7">March 2023</th></tr>
<tr><th>S</th><th>M</th><th>T</th><th>W</th><th>TH</th><th>F</th><th>S</th></tr>
<tr><td></td><td></td><td></td><td>1</td><td>2</td><td>3</td><td>4</td></tr>
<tr><td>5</td><td>6</td><td>7</td><td>8</td><td>9</td><td>10</td><td>11</td></tr>
<tr><td>12</td><td>13</td><td>14</td><td>15</td><td>16</td><td>17</td><td>18</td></tr>
<tr><td>19</td><td>20</td><td>21</td><td>22</td><td>23</td><td>24</td><td>25</td></tr>
<tr><td>26</td><td>27</td><td>28</td><td>29</td><td>30</td><td>31</td><td></td></tr>
</table>

## 2023

# FEB-MAR

**Sunday** 26

**Monday** 27

**Tuesday** 28

**Wednesday 1**

**Thursday 2**

**Friday 3**

**Saturday 4**

## To-Do List

✓

| March 2023 | | | | | | |
|---|---|---|---|---|---|---|
| S | M | T | W | TH | F | S |
| | | | 1 | 2 | 3 | 4 |
| 5 | 6 | 7 | 8 | 9 | 10 | 11 |
| 12 | 13 | 14 | 15 | 16 | 17 | 18 |
| 19 | 20 | 21 | 22 | 23 | 24 | 25 |
| 26 | 27 | 28 | 29 | 30 | 31 | |

| April 2023 | | | | | | |
|---|---|---|---|---|---|---|
| S | M | T | W | TH | F | S |
| | | | | | | 1 |
| 2 | 3 | 4 | 5 | 6 | 7 | 8 |
| 9 | 10 | 11 | 12 | 13 | 14 | 15 |
| 16 | 17 | 18 | 19 | 20 | 21 | 22 |
| 23 | 24 | 25 | 26 | 27 | 28 | 29 |
| 30 | | | | | | |

# 2023
# MARCH

**Sunday** 5

**Monday** 6

**Tuesday** 7  Purim

**Wednesday** 8

**Thursday** 9

**Friday** 10

**Saturday** 11

## To-Do List

✓

## 2023

# MARCH

## Shopping List

✓

---

**Sunday 12** Daylight Saving Time Begins

**Monday 13** Commonwealth Day (Canada)

**Tuesday 14**

**Wednesday** 15

**Thursday** 16

**Friday** 17 St. Patrick's Day

**Saturday** 18

## To-Do List

✓

## Shopping List



## 2023

# MARCH

**Sunday** 19

**Monday** 20  First Day of Spring

**Tuesday** 21

**Wednesday** 22

**Thursday** 23

**Friday** 24

**Saturday** 25

To-Do List

✓

## 2023

# MAR–APR

## Shopping List

✓

**Sunday** 26

**Monday** 27

**Tuesday** 28

**Wednesday** 29

**Thursday** 30

**Friday** 31

**Saturday** 1

## To-Do List

| ✓ |
|---|

# Inviting Jesus In

*But they urged him strongly,*
*"Stay with us."*                    LUKE 24:29

Our last guest said goodbye, and I breathed a sigh of thanks. The Easter dinner we'd planned for family and friends ended on a happy note. Enough food. Good fellowship. No arguments! Over the next days, however, why did I feel a letdown? The holiest day in the Christian calendar—Resurrection Sunday—had blessed our family and friends through our risen Savior. But now, after His resurrection, what should happen next?

For an inspiring answer, the Bible provides a remarkable encounter between Jesus and two believers after His resurrection. The two men—one named Cleopas and the other unnamed—felt let down as they walked from Jerusalem to Emmaus. Still dismayed about Jesus' crucifixion, they were talking when "Jesus himself came up and walked along with them" (Luke 24:13–15).

They didn't recognize Him at first. But what followed was a heartfelt conversation as Jesus challenged the men to have faith in their Messiah's victory—just as the Scriptures prophesied. Their hearts warmed and encouraged, they couldn't let Jesus depart. Instead, a grateful Cleopas invited Christ to come inside and "stay with them" (v. 29).

The triumph of Easter won't fade if we invite Jesus to come inside and stay—at the table of our hearts, where relationships form. He will indwell us with His Spirit—His power present and active in our lives. And when we invite Him, He answers yes!                    LINDA WASHINGTON

# APRIL

| Sunday | Monday | Tuesday | Wednesday |
|---|---|---|---|
|  |  |  |  |
| 2<br>Palm Sunday | 3 | 4 | 5 |
| 9<br>Easter Sunday | 10<br>Easter Monday<br>(Canada) | 11 | 12 |
| 16 | 17 | 18 | 19 |
| 23 / 30 | 24 | 25 | 26 |

*As high as the heavens are above the earth, so great
is his love for those who fear him.*   —PSALM 103:11

| Thursday | Friday | Saturday | Notes |
|---|---|---|---|
| | | 1 | |
| 6<br><br>Maundy Thursday<br>Passover Begins | 7<br><br>Good Friday | 8 | |
| 13<br><br>Passover Ends | 14 | 15 | |
| 20 | 21 | 22<br><br>Earth Day | |
| 27 | 28 | 29 | |

## Shopping List

| April 2023 | | | | | | |
|---|---|---|---|---|---|---|
| S | M | T | W | TH | F | S |
| | | | | | | 1 |
| 2 | 3 | 4 | 5 | 6 | 7 | 8 |
| 9 | 10 | 11 | 12 | 13 | 14 | 15 |
| 16 | 17 | 18 | 19 | 20 | 21 | 22 |
| 23 | 24 | 25 | 26 | 27 | 28 | 29 |
| 30 | | | | | | |

| May 2023 | | | | | | |
|---|---|---|---|---|---|---|
| S | M | T | W | TH | F | S |
| | 1 | 2 | 3 | 4 | 5 | 6 |
| 7 | 8 | 9 | 10 | 11 | 12 | 13 |
| 14 | 15 | 16 | 17 | 18 | 19 | 20 |
| 21 | 22 | 23 | 24 | 25 | 26 | 27 |
| 28 | 29 | 30 | 31 | | | |

## 2023

# APRIL

**Sunday 2** Palm Sunday

**Monday 3**

**Tuesday 4**

**Wednesday** 5

**Thursday** 6 Maundy Thursday
Passover Begins

**Friday** 7 Good Friday

**Saturday** 8

## To-Do List

✓

## 2023

# APRIL

## Shopping List

✓

---

**Sunday** 9 Easter Sunday

---

**Monday** 10 Easter Monday (Canada)

---

**Tuesday** 11

**Wednesday** 12

**Thursday** 13 Passover Ends

**Friday** 14

**Saturday** 15

## To-Do List

✓

## Shopping List

✓

# 2023

# APRIL

**Sunday 16**

**Monday 17**

**Tuesday 18**

**Wednesday** 19

**Thursday** 20

**Friday** 21

**Saturday** 22  Earth Day

## To-Do List

✓

## Shopping List

<table>
<tr><td>April 2023</td></tr>
</table>

| April 2023 | | | | | | |
|---|---|---|---|---|---|---|
| S | M | T | W | TH | F | S |
|  |  |  |  |  |  | 1 |
| 2 | 3 | 4 | 5 | 6 | 7 | 8 |
| 9 | 10 | 11 | 12 | 13 | 14 | 15 |
| 16 | 17 | 18 | 19 | 20 | 21 | 22 |
| 23 | 24 | 25 | 26 | 27 | 28 | 29 |
| 30 |  |  |  |  |  |  |

| May 2023 | | | | | | |
|---|---|---|---|---|---|---|
| S | M | T | W | TH | F | S |
|  | 1 | 2 | 3 | 4 | 5 | 6 |
| 7 | 8 | 9 | 10 | 11 | 12 | 13 |
| 14 | 15 | 16 | 17 | 18 | 19 | 20 |
| 21 | 22 | 23 | 24 | 25 | 26 | 27 |
| 28 | 29 | 30 | 31 |  |  |  |

## 2023
# APRIL

**Sunday** 23

**Monday** 24

**Tuesday** 25

**Wednesday** 26

**Thursday** 27

**Friday** 28

**Saturday** 29

To-Do List

✓

# The Birds in the Temple

*Even the sparrow has found a home . . .
a place near your altar.*     PSALM 84:3

The day after John McCrae lost a friend in World War I, he recorded his thoughts on a notepad. With his friend's freshly dug grave literally in sight, McCrae breathed life into the poem "In Flanders Fields." The opening verse describes "the larks, still bravely singing" as they soared above the din of battle and the crosses marking the graves.

I've rarely seen a goose completely alone like my lonesome feathered friend. Geese are notably communal, flying in a V-formation to deflect the wind. They're made to be together.

It may seem odd to include a description of birds in the chaos of a war scene, but that's what poets do. Their eye for detail and irony captures a fuller picture for us.

An unnamed Hebrew poet included similar details when he wrote about the temple in Jerusalem. The writer himself may have endured the turmoil of war and displacement. "How lovely is your dwelling place, Lord Almighty!" (Psalm 84:1) he exclaimed before pivoting his poet's eye to—*birds.* "Even the sparrow has found a home," he sang, "and the swallow a nest for herself, where she may have her young— a place near your altar" (v. 3).

John McCrae turned his pensive thoughts into a rallying cry for courage to honor the dead amid the carnage of war. The psalmist converted his observations into memorable imagery that points us to the living God. The birds in the temple symbolize what our hearts long for— *a place near His altar.*     TIM GUSTAFSON

*Photo: Holland, Michigan, USA*
*© Terry Bidgood*

2023

# MAY

| Sunday | Monday | Tuesday | Wednesday |
|---|---|---|---|
|  | 1 | 2 | 3 |
| 7 | 8 | 9 | 10 |
| 14 | 15 | 16 | 17 |
| Mother's Day |  |  |  |
| 21 | 22 | 23 | 24 |
|  | Victoria Day (Canada) |  |  |
| 28 | 29 | 30 | 31 |
| Pentecost | Memorial Day |  |  |

| Thursday | Friday | Saturday | Notes |
|---|---|---|---|
| 4<br><br>National Day of Prayer | 5 | 6 | |
| 11 | 12 | 13 | |
| 18<br><br>Ascension Day | 19 | 20 | |
| 25 | 26<br><br>Shavuot | 27 | |
| | | | |

Shopping List

### April 2023

| S | M | T | W | TH | F | S |
|---|---|---|---|---|---|---|
|   |   |   |   |   |   | 1 |
| 2 | 3 | 4 | 5 | 6 | 7 | 8 |
| 9 | 10 | 11 | 12 | 13 | 14 | 15 |
| 16 | 17 | 18 | 19 | 20 | 21 | 22 |
| 23 | 24 | 25 | 26 | 27 | 28 | 29 |
| 30 |   |   |   |   |   |   |

### May 2023

| S | M | T | W | TH | F | S |
|---|---|---|---|---|---|---|
|   | 1 | 2 | 3 | 4 | 5 | 6 |
| 7 | 8 | 9 | 10 | 11 | 12 | 13 |
| 14 | 15 | 16 | 17 | 18 | 19 | 20 |
| 21 | 22 | 23 | 24 | 25 | 26 | 27 |
| 28 | 29 | 30 | 31 |   |   |   |

## 2023

# APR-MAY

**Sunday** 30

**Monday** 1

**Tuesday** 2

**Wednesday** 3

**Thursday** 4  National Day of Prayer

**Friday** 5

**Saturday** 6

## To-Do List

✓

## Shopping List

# 2023

# MAY

**Sunday 7**

**Monday 8**

**Tuesday 9**

**Wednesday** 10

**Thursday** 11

**Friday** 12

**Saturday** 13

To-Do List

✓

## Shopping List

✓

# 2023

# MAY

**Sunday 14** Mother's Day

**Monday 15**

**Tuesday 16**

**Wednesday 17**

**Thursday 18** Ascension Day

**Friday 19**

**Saturday 20**

## To-Do List

✓

## Shopping List

<table>
<tr><td colspan="8" align="center">**May 2023**</td></tr>
<tr><td>S</td><td>M</td><td>T</td><td>W</td><td>TH</td><td>F</td><td>S</td></tr>
<tr><td></td><td>1</td><td>2</td><td>3</td><td>4</td><td>5</td><td>6</td></tr>
<tr><td>7</td><td>8</td><td>9</td><td>10</td><td>11</td><td>12</td><td>13</td></tr>
<tr><td>14</td><td>15</td><td>16</td><td>17</td><td>18</td><td>19</td><td>20</td></tr>
<tr><td>21</td><td>22</td><td>23</td><td>24</td><td>25</td><td>26</td><td>27</td></tr>
<tr><td>28</td><td>29</td><td>30</td><td>31</td><td></td><td></td><td></td></tr>
</table>

<table>
<tr><td colspan="8" align="center">**June 2023**</td></tr>
<tr><td>S</td><td>M</td><td>T</td><td>W</td><td>TH</td><td>F</td><td>S</td></tr>
<tr><td></td><td></td><td></td><td></td><td>1</td><td>2</td><td>3</td></tr>
<tr><td>4</td><td>5</td><td>6</td><td>7</td><td>8</td><td>9</td><td>10</td></tr>
<tr><td>11</td><td>12</td><td>13</td><td>14</td><td>15</td><td>16</td><td>17</td></tr>
<tr><td>18</td><td>19</td><td>20</td><td>21</td><td>22</td><td>23</td><td>24</td></tr>
<tr><td>25</td><td>26</td><td>27</td><td>28</td><td>29</td><td>30</td><td></td></tr>
</table>

# 2023
# MAY

**Sunday** 21

**Monday** 22 Victoria Day (Canada)

**Tuesday** 23

**Wednesday** 24

**Thursday** 25

**Friday** 26 Shavuot

**Saturday** 27

## To-Do List

## Shopping List

✓

<br>

**May 2023**

| S | M | T | W | TH | F | S |
|---|---|---|---|----|---|---|
|   | 1 | 2 | 3 | 4 | 5 | 6 |
| 7 | 8 | 9 | 10 | 11 | 12 | 13 |
| 14 | 15 | 16 | 17 | 18 | 19 | 20 |
| 21 | 22 | 23 | 24 | 25 | 26 | 27 |
| 28 | 29 | 30 | 31 |   |   |   |

**June 2023**

| S | M | T | W | TH | F | S |
|---|---|---|---|----|---|---|
|   |   |   |   | 1 | 2 | 3 |
| 4 | 5 | 6 | 7 | 8 | 9 | 10 |
| 11 | 12 | 13 | 14 | 15 | 16 | 17 |
| 18 | 19 | 20 | 21 | 22 | 23 | 24 |
| 25 | 26 | 27 | 28 | 29 | 30 |   |

## 2023

# MAY–JUN

**Sunday 28** Pentecost

**Monday 29** Memorial Day

**Tuesday 30**

# Wednesday 31

# Thursday 1

# Friday 2

# Saturday 3

## To-Do List

# Jesus Loves Me

*How can I give you up, Ephraim? How can I hand you over, Israel?*　　HOSEA 11:8

For nine weeks, Dan endured beatings and solitary confinement in a foreign jail. He lost hope and tried to kill himself. Four times. After the last failure he slumped to the floor and wept, ashamed of his weakness both to suffer for Jesus and to end his life.

Then a glorious light engulfed his tiny cell. Dan believes he heard the voice of Jesus saying that He still loved and wanted him. *Jesus loves me even when I've lost hope?* Inspired by Jesus' compassion, Dan turned his ensuing (and unjust) trial into a sermon, telling the judge, lawyers, and police how much Jesus loves them.

We may not ever experience something such as Dan did, but we can enjoy Jesus' same promise of love. In Hosea 11, God told His wayward people that He would never quit on them. "How can I give you up, Ephraim? . . . My heart is changed within me; all my compassion is aroused" (v. 8). He said He was patient with them because He was "God, and not a man—the Holy One among you" (v. 9). In Hebrews, God shared why He loves us in our weakness: His Son who came to earth as a man. Jesus "is able to deal gently with those who are ignorant and are going astray" (5:2), since He "has been tempted in every way, just as we are" (4:15).

You may feel weak and broken, but one thing hasn't changed. Jesus understands; He still loves and wants you.　　MIKE WITTMER

*Photo: Riviera Maya, Yucatán Peninsula, on the Caribbean shoreline © Terry Bidgood*

# 2023

# JUNE

| Sunday | Monday | Tuesday | Wednesday |
|---|---|---|---|
|  |  |  |  |
| 4 | 5 | 6 | 7 |
| 11 | 12 | 13 | 14<br>Flag Day (US) |
| 18<br>Father's Day | 19<br>Juneteenth | 20 | 21<br>First Day of Summer |
| 25 | 26 | 27 | 28 |

| Thursday | Friday | Saturday | Notes |
|---|---|---|---|
| 1 | 2 | 3 | |
| 8 | 9 | 10 | |
| 15 | 16 | 17 | |
| 22 | 23 | 24<br>St. Jean Baptiste Day<br>(Canada) | |
| 29 | 30 | | |

## Shopping List

| | June 2023 | | | | | | |
|---|---|---|---|---|---|---|---|
| **S** | **M** | **T** | **W** | **TH** | **F** | **S** |
| | | | | 1 | 2 | 3 |
| 4 | 5 | 6 | 7 | 8 | 9 | 10 |
| 11 | 12 | 13 | 14 | 15 | 16 | 17 |
| 18 | 19 | 20 | 21 | 22 | 23 | 24 |
| 25 | 26 | 27 | 28 | 29 | 30 | |

| July 2023 | | | | | | |
|---|---|---|---|---|---|---|
| **S** | **M** | **T** | **W** | **TH** | **F** | **S** |
| | | | | | | 1 |
| 2 | 3 | 4 | 5 | 6 | 7 | 8 |
| 9 | 10 | 11 | 12 | 13 | 14 | 15 |
| 16 | 17 | 18 | 19 | 20 | 21 | 22 |
| 23 | 24 | 25 | 26 | 27 | 28 | 29 |
| 30 | 31 | | | | | |

## 2023

# JUNE

**Sunday 4**

**Monday 5**

**Tuesday 6**

**Wednesday** 7

**Thursday** 8

**Friday** 9

**Saturday** 10

To-Do List

✓

## Shopping List

| June 2023 |||||||
|---|---|---|---|---|---|---|
| S | M | T | W | TH | F | S |
| | | | | 1 | 2 | 3 |
| 4 | 5 | 6 | 7 | 8 | 9 | 10 |
| 11 | 12 | 13 | 14 | 15 | 16 | 17 |
| 18 | 19 | 20 | 21 | 22 | 23 | 24 |
| 25 | 26 | 27 | 28 | 29 | 30 | |

| July 2023 |||||||
|---|---|---|---|---|---|---|
| S | M | T | W | TH | F | S |
| | | | | | | 1 |
| 2 | 3 | 4 | 5 | 6 | 7 | 8 |
| 9 | 10 | 11 | 12 | 13 | 14 | 15 |
| 16 | 17 | 18 | 19 | 20 | 21 | 22 |
| 23 | 24 | 25 | 26 | 27 | 28 | 29 |
| 30 | 31 | | | | | |

# 2023

# JUNE

**Sunday 11**

**Monday 12**

**Tuesday 13**

**Wednesday 14** Flag Day (US)

**Thursday 15**

**Friday 16**

**Saturday 17**

## To-Do List

✓

## Shopping List

✓

2023

# JUNE

**Sunday 18** Father's Day

**Monday 19** Juneteenth

**Tuesday 20**

**Wednesday 21** First Day of Summer

**Thursday 22**

**Friday 23**

**Saturday 24** St. Jean Baptiste Day
(Canada)

## To-Do List

✓

## Shopping List

<table>
<tr><td>✓</td><td></td></tr>
</table>

| June 2023 | | | | | | |
|---|---|---|---|---|---|---|
| S | M | T | W | TH | F | S |
| | | | | 1 | 2 | 3 |
| 4 | 5 | 6 | 7 | 8 | 9 | 10 |
| 11 | 12 | 13 | 14 | 15 | 16 | 17 |
| 18 | 19 | 20 | 21 | 22 | 23 | 24 |
| 25 | 26 | 27 | 28 | 29 | 30 | |

| July 2023 | | | | | | |
|---|---|---|---|---|---|---|
| S | M | T | W | TH | F | S |
| | | | | | | 1 |
| 2 | 3 | 4 | 5 | 6 | 7 | 8 |
| 9 | 10 | 11 | 12 | 13 | 14 | 15 |
| 16 | 17 | 18 | 19 | 20 | 21 | 22 |
| 23 | 24 | 25 | 26 | 27 | 28 | 29 |
| 30 | 31 | | | | | |

## 2023

# JUN-JUL

**Sunday** 25

**Monday** 26

**Tuesday** 27

**Wednesday** 28

**Thursday** 29

**Friday** 30

**Saturday** 1 Canada Day

## To-Do List

✓

# The Roaring Lion

*Be alert and of sober mind. Your enemy the devil prowls around like a roaring lion looking for someone to devour.*

**1 PETER 5:8**

A bear cub is alone on a grassy knoll when a mountain lion spies the cub, roars, charges, and pursues it. Finding itself cornered, the young bear faces its pursuer, standing as tall as it can on its hind legs and growling. The growl reverberates. Surprisingly, the mountain lion scampers away. Then the bear cub turns around, sees its mother, and runs to her. The mother's hulking presence and roar had frightened the foe.

Like the bear cub in that video, we have someone who seeks our destruction: "[Our] enemy the devil prowls around like a roaring lion looking for someone to devour" (1 Peter 5:8). Satan hopes to "devour" us through deception and suffering (John 8:44; 1 Peter 5:9). But also like that cub, we have someone much stronger and fiercer who has our backs: "The Lord . . . will strengthen [us] and protect [us] from the evil one" (2 Thessalonians 3:3).

Yet, as the apostle Peter states, we have our part to play. We are called to "be alert and of sober mind" to "resist [the devil], standing firm in the faith" (1 Peter 5:8–9). There's no avoiding suffering; in fact, Peter says we should expect it (4:12–19). But in our struggles, God's Spirit is there to strengthen and restore us, making us "strong, firm and steadfast" (5:10). He's watching over us—and one day, we'll be safe in His loving arms for all eternity. ALYSON KIEDA

*Photo: Africa © Terry Bidgood*

# JULY

| Sunday | Monday | Tuesday | Wednesday |
|--------|--------|---------|-----------|
|  |  |  |  |
| 2 | 3 | 4<br><br>Independence Day | 5 |
| 9 | 10 | 11 | 12 |
| 16 | 17 | 18 | 19 |
| 23<br>30 | 24<br>31 | 25 | 26 |

| Thursday | Friday | Saturday | Notes |
|---|---|---|---|
|  |  | 1<br>Canada Day |  |
| 6 | 7 | 8 |  |
| 13 | 14 | 15 |  |
| 20 | 21 | 22 |  |
| 27 | 28 | 29 |  |

## Shopping List

<table>
<tr><td>✓</td></tr>
</table>

| July 2023 | | | | | | |
|---|---|---|---|---|---|---|
| S | M | T | W | TH | F | S |
| | | | | | | 1 |
| 2 | 3 | 4 | 5 | 6 | 7 | 8 |
| 9 | 10 | 11 | 12 | 13 | 14 | 15 |
| 16 | 17 | 18 | 19 | 20 | 21 | 22 |
| 23 | 24 | 25 | 26 | 27 | 28 | 29 |
| 30 | 31 | | | | | |

| August 2023 | | | | | | |
|---|---|---|---|---|---|---|
| S | M | T | W | TH | F | S |
| | | 1 | 2 | 3 | 4 | 5 |
| 6 | 7 | 8 | 9 | 10 | 11 | 12 |
| 13 | 14 | 15 | 16 | 17 | 18 | 19 |
| 20 | 21 | 22 | 23 | 24 | 25 | 26 |
| 27 | 28 | 29 | 30 | 31 | | |

# 2023

# JULY

**Sunday** 2

**Monday** 3

**Tuesday** 4  Independence Day

**Wednesday** 5

**Thursday** 6

**Friday** 7

**Saturday** 8

To-Do List

✓

## Shopping List

| July 2023 | | | | | | |
|---|---|---|---|---|---|---|
| S | M | T | W | TH | F | S |
| | | | | | | 1 |
| 2 | 3 | 4 | 5 | 6 | 7 | 8 |
| 9 | 10 | 11 | 12 | 13 | 14 | 15 |
| 16 | 17 | 18 | 19 | 20 | 21 | 22 |
| 23 | 24 | 25 | 26 | 27 | 28 | 29 |
| 30 | 31 | | | | | |

| August 2023 | | | | | | |
|---|---|---|---|---|---|---|
| S | M | T | W | TH | F | S |
| | | 1 | 2 | 3 | 4 | 5 |
| 6 | 7 | 8 | 9 | 10 | 11 | 12 |
| 13 | 14 | 15 | 16 | 17 | 18 | 19 |
| 20 | 21 | 22 | 23 | 24 | 25 | 26 |
| 27 | 28 | 29 | 30 | 31 | | |

## 2023

# JULY

**Sunday** 9

**Monday** 10

**Tuesday** 11

**Wednesday 12**

**Thursday 13**

**Friday 14**

**Saturday 15**

## To-Do List

✓

## Shopping List

| July 2023 | | | | | | |
|---|---|---|---|---|---|---|
| S | M | T | W | TH | F | S |
| | | | | | | 1 |
| 2 | 3 | 4 | 5 | 6 | 7 | 8 |
| 9 | 10 | 11 | 12 | 13 | 14 | 15 |
| 16 | 17 | 18 | 19 | 20 | 21 | 22 |
| 23 | 24 | 25 | 26 | 27 | 28 | 29 |
| 30 | 31 | | | | | |

| August 2023 | | | | | | |
|---|---|---|---|---|---|---|
| S | M | T | W | TH | F | S |
| | | 1 | 2 | 3 | 4 | 5 |
| 6 | 7 | 8 | 9 | 10 | 11 | 12 |
| 13 | 14 | 15 | 16 | 17 | 18 | 19 |
| 20 | 21 | 22 | 23 | 24 | 25 | 26 |
| 27 | 28 | 29 | 30 | 31 | | |

## 2023

# JULY

**Sunday 16**

**Monday 17**

**Tuesday 18**

**Wednesday** 19

**Thursday** 20

**Friday** 21

**Saturday** 22

To-Do List

## Shopping List

<table>
<tr><td>✓</td><td></td></tr>
</table>

### July 2023

| S | M | T | W | TH | F | S |
|---|---|---|---|---|---|---|
|  |  |  |  |  |  | 1 |
| 2 | 3 | 4 | 5 | 6 | 7 | 8 |
| 9 | 10 | 11 | 12 | 13 | 14 | 15 |
| 16 | 17 | 18 | 19 | 20 | 21 | 22 |
| 23 | 24 | 25 | 26 | 27 | 28 | 29 |
| 30 | 31 |  |  |  |  |  |

### August 2023

| S | M | T | W | TH | F | S |
|---|---|---|---|---|---|---|
|  |  | 1 | 2 | 3 | 4 | 5 |
| 6 | 7 | 8 | 9 | 10 | 11 | 12 |
| 13 | 14 | 15 | 16 | 17 | 18 | 19 |
| 20 | 21 | 22 | 23 | 24 | 25 | 26 |
| 27 | 28 | 29 | 30 | 31 |  |  |

## 2023

# JULY

**Sunday** 23

**Monday** 24

**Tuesday** 25

**Wednesday** 26

**Thursday** 27

**Friday** 28

**Saturday** 29

## To-Do List

✓

# Seed Vault

*But now, Lord, what do I look for? My hope is in you.* **PSALM 39:7**

People use banks as a tool for securing their finances and protecting their financial future. But a different kind of bank in Norway seeks to protect a different kind of future—the future of plant life on Earth. The website croptrust.org describes the Svalbard Global Seed Vault as a "seed bank" where future potential crops are protected in a secure environment. Located in a chain of islands in Norway's Arctic region, "The seed vault is an attempt to ensure against the loss of seeds in other gene-banks during large-scale regional or global crises."

Preparations for the future are wise, yet even our best plans are limited in how much we can safeguard. We simply can't plan for every emergency.

David was battling concerns about his own future when he wrote Psalm 39. As he considered current dangers brought about by "the presence of the wicked" (vv. 1–3), life's brevity (vv. 4–6), and even divine chastening (vv. 9–11), he said, "But now, Lord, what do I look for? My hope is in you" (v. 7).

Our lives on this broken planet will be filled with challenges. Some of those challenges may even be the results of our own unwise choices. But regardless of the source of our troubles, our true hope is always in God. He's more than enough to secure both our future here—and with Him in eternity. BILL CROWDER

*Photo: Tea field outside Jakarta, Indonesia*
*© Terry Bidgood*

# AUGUST

| Sunday | Monday | Tuesday | Wednesday |
| --- | --- | --- | --- |
|  |  | 1 | 2 |
| 6 | 7 | 8 | 9 |
| 13 | 14 | 15 | 16 |
| 20 | 21 | 22 | 23 |
| 27 | 28 | 29 | 30 |

| Thursday | Friday | Saturday | Notes |
|---|---|---|---|
| 3 | 4 | 5 | |
| 10 | 11 | 12 | |
| 17 | 18 | 19 | |
| 24 | 25 | 26 | |
| 31 | | | |

## Shopping List

# 2023

# JUL-AUG

**Sunday 30**

**Monday 31**

**Tuesday 1**

**Wednesday** 2

**Thursday** 3

**Friday** 4

**Saturday** 5

## To-Do List

✓

## Shopping List

| ✓ | |
|---|---|

<br>

### August 2023

| S | M | T | W | TH | F | S |
|---|---|---|---|----|---|---|
| | | 1 | 2 | 3 | 4 | 5 |
| 6 | 7 | 8 | 9 | 10 | 11 | 12 |
| 13 | 14 | 15 | 16 | 17 | 18 | 19 |
| 20 | 21 | 22 | 23 | 24 | 25 | 26 |
| 27 | 28 | 29 | 30 | 31 | | |

### September 2023

| S | M | T | W | TH | F | S |
|---|---|---|---|----|---|---|
| | | | | | 1 | 2 |
| 3 | 4 | 5 | 6 | 7 | 8 | 9 |
| 10 | 11 | 12 | 13 | 14 | 15 | 16 |
| 17 | 18 | 19 | 20 | 21 | 22 | 23 |
| 24 | 25 | 26 | 27 | 28 | 29 | 30 |

## 2023

# AUGUST

**Sunday 6**

**Monday 7**

**Tuesday 8**

**Wednesday** 9

___

**Thursday** 10

___

**Friday** 11

___

**Saturday** 12

To-Do List

## Shopping List

✓

<table>
<tr><th colspan="7">August 2023</th></tr>
<tr><th>S</th><th>M</th><th>T</th><th>W</th><th>TH</th><th>F</th><th>S</th></tr>
<tr><td></td><td></td><td>1</td><td>2</td><td>3</td><td>4</td><td>5</td></tr>
<tr><td>6</td><td>7</td><td>8</td><td>9</td><td>10</td><td>11</td><td>12</td></tr>
<tr><td>13</td><td>14</td><td>15</td><td>16</td><td>17</td><td>18</td><td>19</td></tr>
<tr><td>20</td><td>21</td><td>22</td><td>23</td><td>24</td><td>25</td><td>26</td></tr>
<tr><td>27</td><td>28</td><td>29</td><td>30</td><td>31</td><td></td><td></td></tr>
</table>

<table>
<tr><th colspan="7">September 2023</th></tr>
<tr><th>S</th><th>M</th><th>T</th><th>W</th><th>TH</th><th>F</th><th>S</th></tr>
<tr><td></td><td></td><td></td><td></td><td></td><td>1</td><td>2</td></tr>
<tr><td>3</td><td>4</td><td>5</td><td>6</td><td>7</td><td>8</td><td>9</td></tr>
<tr><td>10</td><td>11</td><td>12</td><td>13</td><td>14</td><td>15</td><td>16</td></tr>
<tr><td>17</td><td>18</td><td>19</td><td>20</td><td>21</td><td>22</td><td>23</td></tr>
<tr><td>24</td><td>25</td><td>26</td><td>27</td><td>28</td><td>29</td><td>30</td></tr>
</table>

## 2023

# AUGUST

**Sunday** 13

**Monday** 14

**Tuesday** 15

**Wednesday** 16

**Thursday** 17

**Friday** 18

**Saturday** 19

## To-Do List

✓

Shopping List

| August 2023 |
| S M T W TH F S |

| S | M | T | W | TH | F | S |
|---|---|---|---|---|---|---|
|  |  |  |  | 1 | 2 | 3 | 4 | 5 |
| 6 | 7 | 8 | 9 | 10 | 11 | 12 |
| 13 | 14 | 15 | 16 | 17 | 18 | 19 |
| 20 | 21 | 22 | 23 | 24 | 25 | 26 |
| 27 | 28 | 29 | 30 | 31 |  |  |

| September 2023 |

| S | M | T | W | TH | F | S |
|---|---|---|---|---|---|---|
|  |  |  |  |  | 1 | 2 |
| 3 | 4 | 5 | 6 | 7 | 8 | 9 |
| 10 | 11 | 12 | 13 | 14 | 15 | 16 |
| 17 | 18 | 19 | 20 | 21 | 22 | 23 |
| 24 | 25 | 26 | 27 | 28 | 29 | 30 |

## 2023

# AUGUST

**Sunday 20**

**Monday 21**

**Tuesday 22**

**Wednesday** 23

**Thursday** 24

**Friday** 25

**Saturday** 26

To-Do List

## Shopping List

## 2023

# AUG-SEP

**Sunday** 27

**Monday** 28

**Tuesday** 29

**Wednesday** 30

**Thursday** 31

**Friday** 1

**Saturday** 2

## To-Do List

✓

# Turn On Your Lamp

*No one lights a lamp and hides it. . . .
Instead, they put it on a stand, so that
those who come in can see the light.*

LUKE 8:16

A lamp often shines through Rick and Rita's window when I take my service dog out at night. One day, I told them how their light breaks through the darkness and brings me comfort on the nights when my chronic pain makes walking painful. Rick said he uses the lamp when reading his Bible and praying for others—including me. I wasn't surprised. They were the first people in our community to invite us into their home for a meal when we moved to the neighborhood. They were the first to invite us to a Bible study. Even before I knew they were fellow believers, I noticed their smiles shining the light of Christ in our neighborhood.

Jesus said, "No one lights a lamp and hides it in a clay jar or puts it under a bed. Instead, they put it on a stand, so that those who come in can see the light" (Luke 8:16). Christ's Spirit living in us spreads the light of His love and hope in this dark world. We can demonstrate our love for God through tangible expressions of love toward people.

Whether we're sharing a smile, a meal, or a kind word—even when people are watching from a distance—God can use our love for others as a lamp that reflects Him and His ways.

XOCHITL DIXON

*Photo: Portugal Coast  © Terry Bidgood*

# SEPTEMBER

| Sunday | Monday | Tuesday | Wednesday |
|---|---|---|---|
|  |  |  |  |
| 3 | 4<br><br>Labor Day<br>Labour Day (Canada) | 5 | 6 |
| 10<br><br>Grandparents Day | 11 | 12 | 13 |
| 17 | 18 | 19 | 20 |
| 24 | 25<br><br>Yom Kippur | 26 | 27 |

*There is no one holy like the LORD; there is no one besides you; there is no Rock like our God.*   —1 SAMUEL 2:2

| Thursday | Friday | Saturday | Notes |
|---|---|---|---|
|  | 1 | 2 |  |
| 7 | 8 | 9 |  |
| 14 | 15 | 16<br>Rosh Hashanah |  |
| 21 | 22 | 23<br>First Day of Autumn |  |
| 28 | 29 | 30<br>Sukkot Begins |  |

## Shopping List

| September 2023 | | | | | | | | October 2023 | | | | | | |
|---|---|---|---|---|---|---|---|---|---|---|---|---|---|---|
| S | M | T | W | TH | F | S | | S | M | T | W | TH | F | S |
| | | | | | 1 | 2 | | 1 | 2 | 3 | 4 | 5 | 6 | 7 |
| 3 | 4 | 5 | 6 | 7 | 8 | 9 | | 8 | 9 | 10 | 11 | 12 | 13 | 14 |
| 10 | 11 | 12 | 13 | 14 | 15 | 16 | | 15 | 16 | 17 | 18 | 19 | 20 | 21 |
| 17 | 18 | 19 | 20 | 21 | 22 | 23 | | 22 | 23 | 24 | 25 | 26 | 27 | 28 |
| 24 | 25 | 26 | 27 | 28 | 29 | 30 | | 29 | 30 | 31 | | | | |

## 2023

# SEPTEMBER

**Sunday** 3

**Monday** 4   Labor Day
Labour Day (Canada)

**Tuesday** 5

**Wednesday** 6

**Thursday** 7

**Friday** 8

**Saturday** 9

## To-Do List

✓

## Shopping List

| September 2023 | | | | | | |
|---|---|---|---|---|---|---|
| S | M | T | W | TH | F | S |
| | | | | | 1 | 2 |
| 3 | 4 | 5 | 6 | 7 | 8 | 9 |
| 10 | 11 | 12 | 13 | 14 | 15 | 16 |
| 17 | 18 | 19 | 20 | 21 | 22 | 23 |
| 24 | 25 | 26 | 27 | 28 | 29 | 30 |

| October 2023 | | | | | | |
|---|---|---|---|---|---|---|
| S | M | T | W | TH | F | S |
| 1 | 2 | 3 | 4 | 5 | 6 | 7 |
| 8 | 9 | 10 | 11 | 12 | 13 | 14 |
| 15 | 16 | 17 | 18 | 19 | 20 | 21 |
| 22 | 23 | 24 | 25 | 26 | 27 | 28 |
| 29 | 30 | 31 | | | | |

## 2023

# SEPTEMBER

**Sunday 10** Grandparents Day

**Monday 11**

**Tuesday 12**

**Wednesday** 13

**Thursday** 14

**Friday** 15

**Saturday** 16 Rosh Hashanah

## To-Do List

✓

## Shopping List

| ✓ | |
|---|---|



| S | M | T | W | TH | F | S |
|---|---|---|---|---|---|---|
| | | | | | 1 | 2 |
| 3 | 4 | 5 | 6 | 7 | 8 | 9 |
| 10 | 11 | 12 | 13 | 14 | 15 | 16 |
| 17 | 18 | 19 | 20 | 21 | 22 | 23 |
| 24 | 25 | 26 | 27 | 28 | 29 | 30 |



| S | M | T | W | TH | F | S |
|---|---|---|---|---|---|---|
| 1 | 2 | 3 | 4 | 5 | 6 | 7 |
| 8 | 9 | 10 | 11 | 12 | 13 | 14 |
| 15 | 16 | 17 | 18 | 19 | 20 | 21 |
| 22 | 23 | 24 | 25 | 26 | 27 | 28 |
| 29 | 30 | 31 | | | | |

2023

# SEPTEMBER

**Sunday** 17

**Monday** 18

**Tuesday** 19

**Wednesday** 20

**Thursday** 21

**Friday** 22

**Saturday** 23   First Day of Autumn

## To-Do List

✓

## Shopping List

2023

# SEPTEMBER

**Sunday 24**

**Monday 25** Yom Kippur

**Tuesday 26**

**Wednesday** 27

**Thursday** 28

**Friday** 29

**Saturday** 30 Sukkot Begins

## To-Do List

✓

# Unshakable Identity

*See what great love the Father has lavished on us, that we should be called children of God! And that is what we are!* 1 JOHN 3:1

After I spoke at a church one night, a man came up to talk. "I don't normally go to church," he said, "and I've never been to this church before. I don't even know why I'm here. I was just walking past and something drew me in. But what you've shared tonight was what I needed to hear."

I'd spoken about how trials like unemployment, illness, and divorce can impact our identity and hinder us from becoming who we've wanted to become, but how the gospel offers an identity we can never lose: being children of God (1 John 3:1–3). I marveled at how this man had been led to hear this message when he most needed it, but I had no idea how true this was. "Tonight I was planning to take my life," he added. "But I won't, because now I'm a child of God!"

Being God's child means in our darkest moments we're not alone (Deuteronomy 31:6), in our poorest times we have a divine inheritance (Ephesians 1:18), and at our worst we have a home to return to (Luke 15:11–32). Close to losing it all, this man was about to receive everything he'd ever needed.

Life can be tough, shaking our identity. But thankfully, when we can't become who we want to be, we can still become who we're meant to be—children of God, an unshakable identity that can literally save our lives.

SHERIDAN VOYSEY

## 2023
# OCTOBER

| Sunday | Monday | Tuesday | Wednesday |
|---|---|---|---|
| 1 | 2 | 3 | 4 |
| 8 | 9<br><br>Columbus Day/<br>Indigenous Peoples' Day<br><br>Thanksgiving Day (Canada) | 10 | 11 |
| 15 | 16 | 17 | 18 |
| 22 | 23 | 24 | 25 |
| 29 | 30 | 31 | |

*There is a time for everything, and a season for every activity under the heavens.* —ECCLESIASTES 3:1

| Thursday | Friday | Saturday | Notes |
|---|---|---|---|
| 5 | 6 | 7 | |
| | Sukkot Ends | | |
| 12 | 13 | 14 | |
| 19 | 20 | 21 | |
| 26 | 27 | 28 | |
| | | | |

## Shopping List

✓

# 2023

# OCTOBER

**Sunday** 1

**Monday** 2

**Tuesday** 3

**Wednesday** 4

**Thursday** 5

**Friday** 6 Sukkot Ends

**Saturday** 7

## To-Do List

## Shopping List

2023

# OCTOBER

**Sunday** 8

**Monday** 9   Columbus Day/Indigenous Peoples' Day
Thanksgiving Day (Canada)

**Tuesday** 10

**Wednesday** 11

**Thursday** 12

**Friday** 13

**Saturday** 14

## To-Do List

✓

| October 2023 | | | | | | |
|---|---|---|---|---|---|---|
| S | M | T | W | TH | F | S |
| 1 | 2 | 3 | 4 | 5 | 6 | 7 |
| 8 | 9 | 10 | 11 | 12 | 13 | 14 |
| 15 | 16 | 17 | 18 | 19 | 20 | 21 |
| 22 | 23 | 24 | 25 | 26 | 27 | 28 |
| 29 | 30 | 31 | | | | |

| November 2023 | | | | | | |
|---|---|---|---|---|---|---|
| S | M | T | W | TH | F | S |
| | | | 1 | 2 | 3 | 4 |
| 5 | 6 | 7 | 8 | 9 | 10 | 11 |
| 12 | 13 | 14 | 15 | 16 | 17 | 18 |
| 19 | 20 | 21 | 22 | 23 | 24 | 25 |
| 26 | 27 | 28 | 29 | 30 | | |

# 2023
# OCTOBER

**Sunday** 15

**Monday** 16

**Tuesday** 17

**Wednesday** 18

**Thursday** 19

**Friday** 20

**Saturday** 21

## To-Do List

✓

## Shopping List

<table>
<tr><td>✓</td><td></td></tr>
</table>

October 2023

| S | M | T | W | TH | F | S |
|---|---|---|---|----|---|---|
| 1 | 2 | 3 | 4 | 5 | 6 | 7 |
| 8 | 9 | 10 | 11 | 12 | 13 | 14 |
| 15 | 16 | 17 | 18 | 19 | 20 | 21 |
| 22 | 23 | 24 | 25 | 26 | 27 | 28 |
| 29 | 30 | 31 | | | | |

November 2023

| S | M | T | W | TH | F | S |
|---|---|---|---|----|---|---|
| | | | 1 | 2 | 3 | 4 |
| 5 | 6 | 7 | 8 | 9 | 10 | 11 |
| 12 | 13 | 14 | 15 | 16 | 17 | 18 |
| 19 | 20 | 21 | 22 | 23 | 24 | 25 |
| 26 | 27 | 28 | 29 | 30 | | |

## 2023

# OCTOBER

**Sunday** 22

**Monday** 23

**Tuesday** 24

**Wednesday** 25

**Thursday** 26

**Friday** 27

**Saturday** 28

## To-Do List

✓

# Sadness into Smiles

*Praise be to the God and Father of our Lord Jesus Christ, the Father of compassion and the God of all comfort.*

2 CORINTHIANS 1:3

Tragedy struck twice for a little boy named Jaden. When he was four, his father died. Then, not long after that, his mother died in her sleep. Understandably, he was surrounded by a lot of mourning people. But Jaden said he was tired of seeing everybody sad all the time.

So here's what he did, according to a feature on *CBS Evening News*. He asked his guardian to purchase a bunch of little toys—rubber duckies, dinosaurs, and the like. Then she and Jaden went to the nearby city, and he handed them out to people on the street who didn't seem happy. "I'm trying to make people smile," he said. And it worked. Smiles, hugs, and even happy tears resulted.

Jaden may not have been aware of it, but his kind actions are a small picture of what God does for us in times of our own sadness: He brings comfort. "The Lord is close to the brokenhearted," wrote David (Psalm 34:18); and another psalmist penned, "he heals the brokenhearted and binds up their wounds" (Psalm 147:3). God "comforts us in all our troubles," reminds Paul (2 Corinthians 1:4).

In life's times of sadness, we know Someone who cares deeply for us. He's the "Father of compassion and the God of all comfort" (v. 3). Even through our pain we can find hope because of Paul's reminder that "our comfort abounds through Christ" (v. 5). DAVE BRANON

*Photo: 140-year-old Hofskirkja Church, southeast Iceland  © Terry Bidgood*

# NOVEMBER

| Sunday | Monday | Tuesday | Wednesday |
|---|---|---|---|
| | | | 1 |
| 5<br><br>Daylight Saving Time Ends | 6 | 7 | 8 |
| 12 | 13 | 14 | 15 |
| 19 | 20 | 21 | 22 |
| 26 | 27 | 28 | 29 |

| Thursday | Friday | Saturday | Notes |
|---|---|---|---|
| 2 | 3 | 4 | |
| 9 | 10 | 11<br>Veterans Day<br>Remembrance Day (Canada) | |
| 16 | 17 | 18 | |
| 23<br>Thanksgiving Day | 24 | 25 | |
| 30 | | | |

## Shopping List

✓

# 2023

# OCT–NOV

**Sunday** 29

**Monday** 30

**Tuesday** 31

**Wednesday** 1

**Thursday** 2

**Friday** 3

**Saturday** 4

To-Do List

Shopping List

✓

<table>
<tr><td colspan="8" align="center">November 2023</td></tr>
<tr><td>S</td><td>M</td><td>T</td><td>W</td><td>TH</td><td>F</td><td>S</td></tr>
<tr><td></td><td></td><td></td><td>1</td><td>2</td><td>3</td><td>4</td></tr>
<tr><td>5</td><td>6</td><td>7</td><td>8</td><td>9</td><td>10</td><td>11</td></tr>
<tr><td>12</td><td>13</td><td>14</td><td>15</td><td>16</td><td>17</td><td>18</td></tr>
<tr><td>19</td><td>20</td><td>21</td><td>22</td><td>23</td><td>24</td><td>25</td></tr>
<tr><td>26</td><td>27</td><td>28</td><td>29</td><td>30</td><td></td><td></td></tr>
</table>

<table>
<tr><td colspan="8" align="center">December 2023</td></tr>
<tr><td>S</td><td>M</td><td>T</td><td>W</td><td>TH</td><td>F</td><td>S</td></tr>
<tr><td></td><td></td><td></td><td></td><td></td><td>1</td><td>2</td></tr>
<tr><td>3</td><td>4</td><td>5</td><td>6</td><td>7</td><td>8</td><td>9</td></tr>
<tr><td>10</td><td>11</td><td>12</td><td>13</td><td>14</td><td>15</td><td>16</td></tr>
<tr><td>17</td><td>18</td><td>19</td><td>20</td><td>21</td><td>22</td><td>23</td></tr>
<tr><td>24</td><td>25</td><td>26</td><td>27</td><td>28</td><td>29</td><td>30</td></tr>
<tr><td>31</td><td></td><td></td><td></td><td></td><td></td><td></td></tr>
</table>

## 2023

# NOVEMBER

**Sunday 5** Daylight Saving Time Ends

**Monday 6**

**Tuesday 7**

**Wednesday** 8

**Thursday** 9

**Friday** 10

**Saturday** 11 Veterans Day
Remembrance Day (Canada)

## To-Do List

✓

## Shopping List

<table>
<tr><td>November 2023</td><td>December 2023</td></tr>
</table>

**November 2023**

| S | M | T | W | TH | F | S |
|---|---|---|---|----|---|---|
|   |   |   | 1 | 2  | 3 | 4 |
| 5 | 6 | 7 | 8 | 9  | 10 | 11 |
| 12 | 13 | 14 | 15 | 16 | 17 | 18 |
| 19 | 20 | 21 | 22 | 23 | 24 | 25 |
| 26 | 27 | 28 | 29 | 30 |   |   |

**December 2023**

| S | M | T | W | TH | F | S |
|---|---|---|---|----|---|---|
|   |   |   |   |   | 1 | 2 |
| 3 | 4 | 5 | 6 | 7 | 8 | 9 |
| 10 | 11 | 12 | 13 | 14 | 15 | 16 |
| 17 | 18 | 19 | 20 | 21 | 22 | 23 |
| 24 | 25 | 26 | 27 | 28 | 29 | 30 |
| 31 |   |   |   |   |   |   |

## 2023

# NOVEMBER

**Sunday 12**

**Monday 13**

**Tuesday 14**

**Wednesday 15**

**Thursday 16**

**Friday 17**

**Saturday 18**

## To-Do List

## Shopping List

✓

| November 2023 | | | | | | |
|---|---|---|---|---|---|---|
| S | M | T | W | TH | F | S |
| | | | 1 | 2 | 3 | 4 |
| 5 | 6 | 7 | 8 | 9 | 10 | 11 |
| 12 | 13 | 14 | 15 | 16 | 17 | 18 |
| 19 | 20 | 21 | 22 | 23 | 24 | 25 |
| 26 | 27 | 28 | 29 | 30 | | |

| December 2023 | | | | | | |
|---|---|---|---|---|---|---|
| S | M | T | W | TH | F | S |
| | | | | | 1 | 2 |
| 3 | 4 | 5 | 6 | 7 | 8 | 9 |
| 10 | 11 | 12 | 13 | 14 | 15 | 16 |
| 17 | 18 | 19 | 20 | 21 | 22 | 23 |
| 24 | 25 | 26 | 27 | 28 | 29 | 30 |
| 31 | | | | | | |

## 2023

# NOVEMBER

**Sunday** 19

**Monday** 20

**Tuesday** 21

**Wednesday** 22

**Thursday** 23 Thanksgiving Day

**Friday** 24

**Saturday** 25

## To-Do List

✓

## Shopping List

✓

<br>

| November 2023 | | | | | | |
|---|---|---|---|---|---|---|
| S | M | T | W | TH | F | S |
| | | | 1 | 2 | 3 | 4 |
| 5 | 6 | 7 | 8 | 9 | 10 | 11 |
| 12 | 13 | 14 | 15 | 16 | 17 | 18 |
| 19 | 20 | 21 | 22 | 23 | 24 | 25 |
| 26 | 27 | 28 | 29 | 30 | | |

| December 2023 | | | | | | |
|---|---|---|---|---|---|---|
| S | M | T | W | TH | F | S |
| | | | | | 1 | 2 |
| 3 | 4 | 5 | 6 | 7 | 8 | 9 |
| 10 | 11 | 12 | 13 | 14 | 15 | 16 |
| 17 | 18 | 19 | 20 | 21 | 22 | 23 |
| 24 | 25 | 26 | 27 | 28 | 29 | 30 |
| 31 | | | | | | |

## 2023

# NOV-DEC

**Sunday** 26

**Monday** 27

**Tuesday** 28

**Wednesday** 29

**Thursday** 30

**Friday** 1

**Saturday** 2

To-Do List

# Beckoned to Worship

*Come, let us bow down in worship.*

**PSALM 95:6**

Kathryn invited her family, friends, fellow Scots, and everyone around the world to step outside and join her in two minutes of bell-ringing at 6:00 p.m. on Christmas Eve. Her desire was to end a difficult year with some cheer and to create a special moment for children who wondered if Christmas might be different in the midst of a pandemic. Bells have long been associated with Christmas, even more so in some church traditions that use bells to beckon those within hearing to join in worship throughout the year.

Kathryn's invitation resembles the one issued by the psalmist, whose message rings out from the pages of the Bible. He declares a moving call to God's people to worship, inviting both his contemporaries and us to "sing for joy to the Lord" and "extol him with music and song" (Psalm 95:1–2). Despite hardships in their shared history, resulting from hard-heartedness and spiritual straying, the psalmist beckons us back to God, to "bow down in worship" (v. 6) because—despite our wrongdoing—we are His.

When we recognize God's care for us, His greatness, and His creative powers in forming and sustaining the earth, we're moved to thanksgiving and rejoicing. But the act of worship is more than a mere mood-lifter; it reminds us of the unshakable truths of who God is, His matchless power, and His daily presence in our lives—beckoning us back to Him at Christmas and every day.

KRISTEN HOLMBERG

# DECEMBER

| Sunday | Monday | Tuesday | Wednesday |
| --- | --- | --- | --- |
|  |  |  |  |
| 3<br>Advent Begins | 4 | 5 | 6 |
| 10 | 11 | 12 | 13 |
| 17 | 18 | 19 | 20 |
| 24<br>Christmas Eve<br>New Year's Eve 31 | 25<br>Christmas Day | 26<br>Boxing Day (Canada) | 27 |

*Why do you worry about clothes? See how the flowers of the field grow. They do not labor or spin. Yet I tell you that not even Solomon in all his splendor was dressed like one of these.* —MATTHEW 6:28-29

| Thursday | Friday | Saturday | Notes |
|---|---|---|---|
|  | 1 | 2 |  |
| 7 | 8<br>Hanukkah Begins | 9 |  |
| 14 | 15<br>Hanukkah Ends | 16 |  |
| 21<br>First Day of Winter | 22 | 23 |  |
| 28 | 29 | 30 |  |

Shopping List

| December 2023 | | | | | | |
|---|---|---|---|---|---|---|
| S | M | T | W | TH | F | S |
| | | | | | 1 | 2 |
| 3 | 4 | 5 | 6 | 7 | 8 | 9 |
| 10 | 11 | 12 | 13 | 14 | 15 | 16 |
| 17 | 18 | 19 | 20 | 21 | 22 | 23 |
| 24 | 25 | 26 | 27 | 28 | 29 | 30 |
| 31 | | | | | | |

| January 2024 | | | | | | |
|---|---|---|---|---|---|---|
| S | M | T | W | TH | F | S |
| | 1 | 2 | 3 | 4 | 5 | 6 |
| 7 | 8 | 9 | 10 | 11 | 12 | 13 |
| 14 | 15 | 16 | 17 | 18 | 19 | 20 |
| 21 | 22 | 23 | 24 | 25 | 26 | 27 |
| 28 | 29 | 30 | 31 | | | |

## 2023

# DECEMBER

**Sunday 3** Advent Begins

**Monday 4**

**Tuesday 5**

**Wednesday 6**

**Thursday 7**

**Friday 8**  Hanukkah Begins

**Saturday 9**

## To-Do List

✓

## Shopping List

✓

| December 2023 | | | | | | |
|---|---|---|---|---|---|---|
| S | M | T | W | TH | F | S |
| | | | | | 1 | 2 |
| 3 | 4 | 5 | 6 | 7 | 8 | 9 |
| 10 | 11 | 12 | 13 | 14 | 15 | 16 |
| 17 | 18 | 19 | 20 | 21 | 22 | 23 |
| 24 | 25 | 26 | 27 | 28 | 29 | 30 |
| 31 | | | | | | |

| January 2024 | | | | | | |
|---|---|---|---|---|---|---|
| S | M | T | W | TH | F | S |
| | 1 | 2 | 3 | 4 | 5 | 6 |
| 7 | 8 | 9 | 10 | 11 | 12 | 13 |
| 14 | 15 | 16 | 17 | 18 | 19 | 20 |
| 21 | 22 | 23 | 24 | 25 | 26 | 27 |
| 28 | 29 | 30 | 31 | | | |

## 2023

# DECEMBER

**Sunday** 10

**Monday** 11

**Tuesday** 12

**Wednesday** 13

**Thursday** 14

**Friday** 15    Hanukkah Ends

**Saturday** 16

## To-Do List

✓

## Shopping List



| December 2023 | January 2024 |
| --- | --- |

**December 2023**

| S | M | T | W | TH | F | S |
| --- | --- | --- | --- | --- | --- | --- |
|  |  |  |  |  | 1 | 2 |
| 3 | 4 | 5 | 6 | 7 | 8 | 9 |
| 10 | 11 | 12 | 13 | 14 | 15 | 16 |
| 17 | 18 | 19 | 20 | 21 | 22 | 23 |
| 24 | 25 | 26 | 27 | 28 | 29 | 30 |
| 31 |  |  |  |  |  |  |

**January 2024**

| S | M | T | W | TH | F | S |
| --- | --- | --- | --- | --- | --- | --- |
|  | 1 | 2 | 3 | 4 | 5 | 6 |
| 7 | 8 | 9 | 10 | 11 | 12 | 13 |
| 14 | 15 | 16 | 17 | 18 | 19 | 20 |
| 21 | 22 | 23 | 24 | 25 | 26 | 27 |
| 28 | 29 | 30 | 31 |  |  |  |

## 2023

# DECEMBER

**Sunday 17**

**Monday 18**

**Tuesday 19**

**Wednesday** 20

**Thursday** 21    First Day of Winter

**Friday** 22

**Saturday** 23

## To-Do List

✓

## Shopping List

| December 2023 | | | | | | | | | January 2024 | | | | | | |
|---|---|---|---|---|---|---|---|---|---|---|---|---|---|---|
| **S** | **M** | **T** | **W** | **TH** | **F** | **S** | | **S** | **M** | **T** | **W** | **TH** | **F** | **S** |
| | | | | | 1 | 2 | | | 1 | 2 | 3 | 4 | 5 | 6 |
| 3 | 4 | 5 | 6 | 7 | 8 | 9 | | 7 | 8 | 9 | 10 | 11 | 12 | 13 |
| 10 | 11 | 12 | 13 | 14 | 15 | 16 | | 14 | 15 | 16 | 17 | 18 | 19 | 20 |
| 17 | 18 | 19 | 20 | 21 | 22 | 23 | | 21 | 22 | 23 | 24 | 25 | 26 | 27 |
| 24 | 25 | 26 | 27 | 28 | 29 | 30 | | 28 | 29 | 30 | 31 | | | |
| 31 | | | | | | | | | | | | | | |

## 2023

# DECEMBER

**Sunday** 24   Christmas Eve

**Monday** 25   Christmas Day

**Tuesday** 26   Boxing Day (Canada)

**Wednesday** 27

**Thursday** 28

**Friday** 29

**Saturday** 30

## To-Do List

## Shopping List



## 2023–2024

# DEC–JAN

**Sunday 31** New Year's Eve

**Monday 1** New Year's Day

**Tuesday 2**

**Wednesday** 3

**Thursday** 4

**Friday** 5

**Saturday** 6

To-Do List

✓

# IMPORTANT CONTACTS

Name:

Address:

City:                              State:                    Zip:

Mobile Phone:                      Email:

Name:

Address:

City:                              State:                    Zip:

Mobile Phone:                      Email:

Name:

Address:

City:                              State:                    Zip:

Mobile Phone:                      Email:

Name:

Address:

City:                              State:                    Zip:

Mobile Phone:                      Email:

# IMPORTANT CONTACTS

Name:

Address:

City:                          State:              Zip:

Mobile Phone:                  Email:

Name:

Address:

City:                          State:              Zip:

Mobile Phone:                  Email:

Name:

Address:

City:                          State:              Zip:

Mobile Phone:                  Email:

Name:

Address:

City:                          State:              Zip:

Mobile Phone:                  Email:

# IMPORTANT CONTACTS

Name:

Address:

City:                          State:              Zip:

Mobile Phone:                  Email:

Name:

Address:

City:                          State:              Zip:

Mobile Phone:                  Email:

Name:

Address:

City:                          State:              Zip:

Mobile Phone:                  Email:

Name:

Address:

City:                          State:              Zip:

Mobile Phone:                  Email:

# IMPORTANT CONTACTS

Name:

Address:

City:                    State:             Zip:

Mobile Phone:            Email:

Name:

Address:

City:                    State:             Zip:

Mobile Phone:            Email:

Name:

Address:

City:                    State:             Zip:

Mobile Phone:            Email:

Name:

Address:

City:                    State:             Zip:

Mobile Phone:            Email:

# IMPORTANT CONTACTS

Name:

Address:

City:                                    State:                    Zip:

Mobile Phone:                            Email:

Name:

Address:

City:                                    State:                    Zip:

Mobile Phone:                            Email:

Name:

Address:

City:                                    State:                    Zip:

Mobile Phone:                            Email:

Name:

Address:

City:                                    State:                    Zip:

Mobile Phone:                            Email:

# IMPORTANT CONTACTS

Name:

Address:

City:                                State:            Zip:

Mobile Phone:                   Email:

Name:

Address:

City:                                State:            Zip:

Mobile Phone:                   Email:

Name:

Address:

City:                                State:            Zip:

Mobile Phone:                   Email:

Name:

Address:

City:                                State:            Zip:

Mobile Phone:                   Email:

# NOTES

# NOTES

# NOTES

# NOTES

# NOTES

# NOTES

# NOTES

# NOTES

Grow Closer to God Each Day

You can receive your daily devotional by mail, email, web, app, or e-book. Sign up today!

odb.org/subscribe

Our Daily Bread

I will say of the LORD,
"He is my refuge and my fortress,
my God, in whom I trust."

PSALM 91:2

Back
10:16 AM
Our Daily Bread

God at Work
Amy Boucher Pye

May he work in us what is pleasing to him, through Jesus Christ. Hebrews 13:21

Read: Hebrews 13:20–21